NISTIR 7548

Selected Impacts of Documentary Standards Supported by NIST 2008 Edition

Erik Puskar
Standards Coordination and Conformity Group
Standards Services Division
Technology Services

National Institute of Standards and Technology
Gaithersburg, MD 20899

January 2009

U.S. DEPARTMENT OF COMMERCE
Carlos M. Gutierrez, Secretary

NATIONAL INSTITUTE OF STANDARDS AND TECHNOLOGY
Patrick Gallagher, Acting Deputy Director

Table of Contents

List of Acronyms ii
    I.   Executive Summary 1
    II.   Background 3
    III.   Proposed Approach 5
    IV.   Report Methodology 8
    V.   NIST Participation..9
    VI.   Findings..11
    VII. Reported Outcomes 14
    VIII. 16 CFR Part 1633 Standard for the Flammability (Open Flame) of Mattress Sets...18
    IX.   Development of Radiation Detector Standards for Homeland Security Applications..23
    X.   Materials Declaration Standards to Support Environmental Regs 29
    XI.   Future Steps and Conclusion 35

Table of Figures:

Figure 1   NIST Technology Services Created an Approach to Evaluating Stds........1
Figure 2   NIST Involvement in Standards Development 3
Figure 3   Strategic Assessment Development Process...5
Figure 4   Breakdown of Standards Participation by Org. Type 14
Figure 1F Mattress Sets...18
Figure 2F Burning Bed at One and a Half Minutes 21
Figure 1R NIST Technical Leadership Contributes..24
Figure 2R Cargo Screening Equipment Installed at an Airport 25
Figure 3R Handheld Radiation Detectors 27
Figure 1M NIST has Positive Impact on Standards Development............................30
Figure 2M IPC 1752 Tool Screen Shot Showing Class 1 & 2 Declarations..............33

List of Tables:

Table 1   NIST Participation in Standards Committees by OU 10
Table 2   Sample Overview of Impacts Derived from NIST 11
Table 3   Application Areas...13
Table 4   Description of Intermediate Outcome Metrics...14
Table 5   Canvassing Results...37
Table 1R IEEE's Radiation Detection Standards..26

List of Acronyms

ACI	American Concrete Institute
ANSI	American National Standards Institute
ASHRAE	American Society of Heating, Refrigerating and Air-Conditioning Engineers
ASME	American Society for Mechanical Engineers
ASTM	ASTM International, formerly American Society for Testing & Materials
CIE	International Commission on Illumination
CIPM	International Committee for Weights and Measures
CISPR	The International Special Committee on Radio Interference
CLSI	The Clinical and Laboratory Standards Institute
DHS	Department of Homeland Security
DNDO	Domestic Nuclear Detection Office
DOE	Department of Energy
FIPS	Federal Information Processing Standard
GRaDER	Graduated Rad/Nuc Detector Evaluation and Reporting Program
HITSP	Health Information Technology Standards Panel
HL7	Health Level 7
HIS	Homeland Security Instrumentation
IEC	International Electrotechnical Commission
IEEE	Institute of Electronic and Electrical and Electronics Engineers
IESNA	Illuminating Engineering Society of North America
IETF	Internet Engineering Task Force
IFSTA	International Fire Service Training Association
ILO	International Labour Organization
INCITS	International Committee for Information Technology Standards
iNEMI	The International Electronics Manufacturing Initiative
IPC	formerly Institute of Interconnecting and Packaging Electronic Circuits
IT	Information Technology
ISO	International Organization for Standardization

ITU	International Telecommunication Union
JTC1	ISO Joint Technical Committee 1 (Information Technology Standards)
NEMA	National Electronics Manufacturers Association
NFPA	National Fire Protection Association
NIJ	National Institute of Justice
NIST	National Institute of Standards and Technology
NVLAP	National Voluntary Laboratory Accreditation Program
OAG	Open Applications Group
OASIS	Organization for the Advancement of Structured Information Standards.
OIML	International Organization for Legal Metrology
OMG	Object Management Group
RM	Radioactivity Measurements
SAE	SAE International, formerly Society of Automotive Engineers
SCP	Standards Committee Participation Database
SI	International System of Units
SSL	Solid State Lighting
STEP	Standard for the Exchange of Product Model Data
TIA	Telecommunications Industry Association
UL	Underwriters Laboratories Inc.
VESA	Video Electronics Standards Association
W3C	World Wide Web Consortium

I. Executive Summary

This report is intended to reflect NIST's success in meeting its mission, executive guidance, and legislative requirements for developing standards and reporting on the effect of those standards on the manufacturing and service sectors. The survey and study also support a NIST strategic priority to foster more efficient transactions in the domestic and global marketplace through development and use of effective standards by manufacturing and service sectors.

Figure 1 offers an overview of the reasons why evaluating NIST involvement in standards development makes sense and summarizes the approach towards identifying benefits accrued from NIST involvement in standards development.

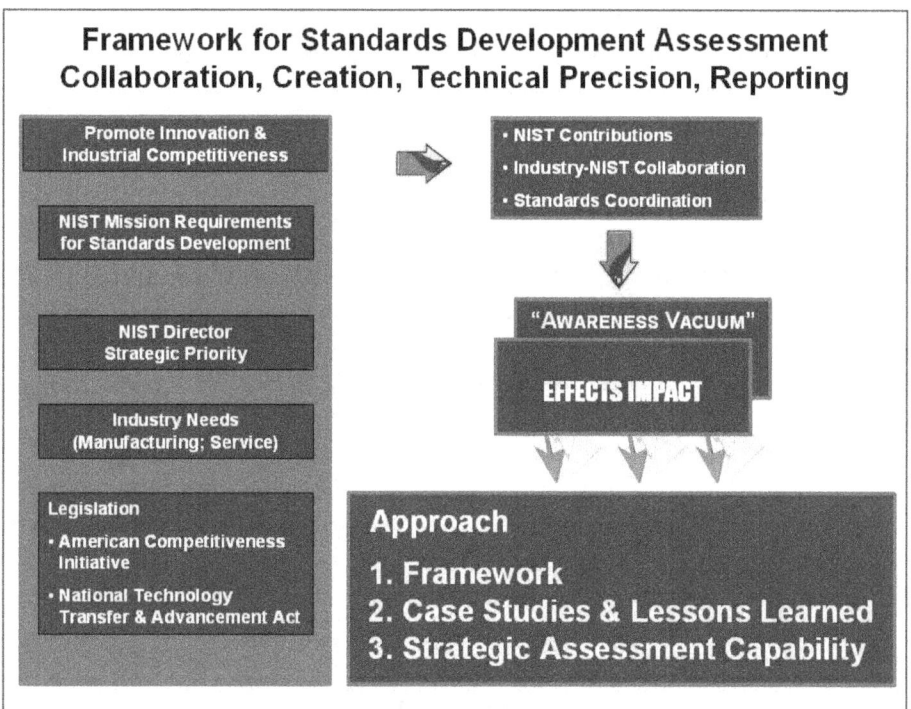

Figure 1: NIST Technology Services Created An Approach to Evaluating Standards Development Impact Based on Policy And NIST Actions

Technology Services canvassed a number of NIST operating units that were involved in recent standards development, obtaining results from 53 of 78 projects. The responses offered some interesting observations and led to a number of implications for NIST involvement in standards development.

The benefits from NIST involvement included producing standards faster than would have been the case without NIST; creating specific improvements to products and services; and developing broader standards. Figure 2 offers highlights of the results. Some specific implications are:

- On average, for every full-time-equivalent of NIST staff working on one of the high impact standards, almost 12 times that amount of non-NIST staff (primarily industry) were supporting the project. This suggests that NIST leverages valuable industry labor, and is indicative of the lower bound estimate of the social benefits of standards development activities.

- NIST participation led to standards produced 1.65 years earlier on average. It is a gross indicator of the transaction time savings that NIST involvement in a voluntary standards development effort affords industry.

- Standards in many cases would have been narrower without NIST involvement. This is a gross indicator of an increase in the number of newly available products or services enabled by the standard in question. Combined with time saving due to NIST's participation, the increase in scope scales up the economic benefits that flow from NIST's participation in voluntary standards development efforts.[1]

- Of 53 projects, 62% had involvement from industry groups or consortia in developing the standard. This percentage indicates strong industry support and, ultimately, significant economic impact.

- Forty-two (42) percent of respondents stated that the standard resulted in having a product or service available, or available at a lower cost, or more broadly, or in different qualities, or earlier that would not be in the absence of the standard. In addition, many of the other respondents, who did not specifically claim new products or services, did claim broader societal benefits, such as: trade facilitation, increased homeland security, interoperability benefits, etc.

- A large majority (85 percent) of the projects resulted in professional publications, including journal articles, conference proceedings and presentations, NIST publications, magazine articles and other reports. These publications are a non-economic indicator of the secondary output of NIST's engagement.

- Of those 23 projects which reported claims that the standard has had an impact on actual products and services, there is a higher ratio of non-NIST participants to NIST staff (15.3 v 11.8). This indicates a higher rate of external (likely industry) participation.

Taken together, it is clear that many of these NIST standards projects leveraged the work of non-NIST participants to develop high impact standards which were developed faster and resulted in product and service improvements and general benefits to the country. If we look at the subsets, industry involvement is, as expected, associated with a larger percentage of new or improved products/services. No attempt has been made yet to put an economic value on the resulting goods and services or the faster development time.

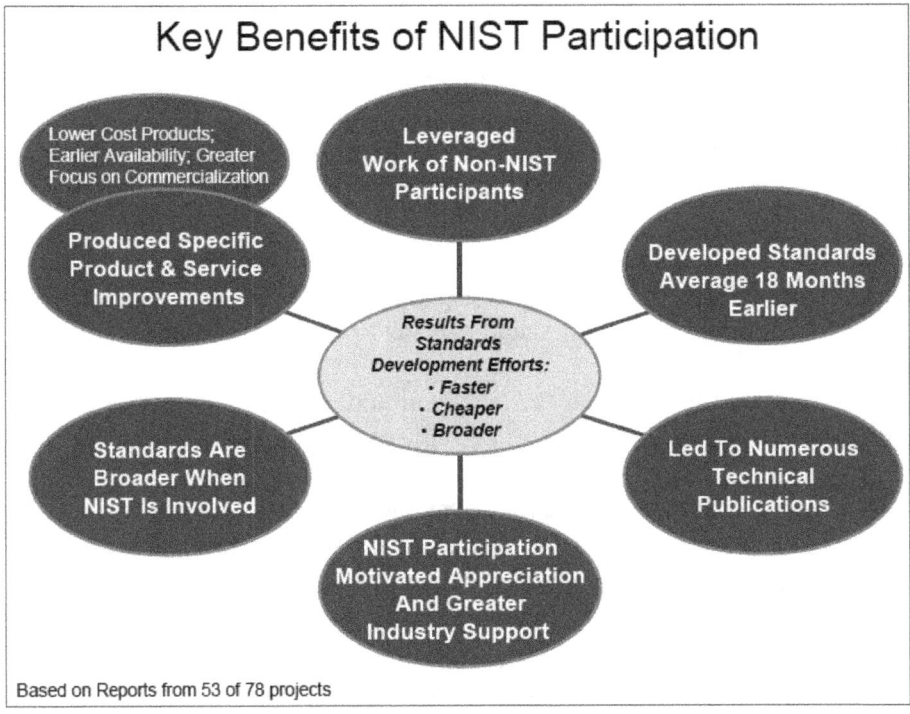

Figure 2: NIST Involvement In Standards Development Generates A Range of Benefits for Industry

NIST involvement in voluntary standards development efforts need not result in new products or services to generate significant economic impacts. The only basic requirement is that NIST bring valuable resources to a process that contributes value to the marketplace of producers and consumers. Where new products and services are available, additional benefit streams will have been induced. Where NIST contributes uniquely to the flow of those benefits, the returns to the investment of NIST's resources will be higher yet.[2]

II. Background

The mission of the National Institute of Standards and Technology (NIST) is to promote U.S. innovation and industrial competitiveness. One of NIST's core competencies is the development and use of standards. During late 2007, Technology Services (TS) canvassed other NIST Operating Units (OUs) to answer the question: How well is NIST doing in this area? The OUs were specifically asked about instances where NIST has played an active role in the development or implementation of documentary standards that:
     (1) have been broadly adopted, or
     (2) have produced, or are expected to produce, significant economic or societal benefits.

This study reports on the results of the survey.[1] The report is intended to reflect NIST's success in meeting its mission, executive guidance, and legislative requirements for developing standards and reporting on the effect of those standards on the manufacturing and service sectors. The survey and study also support one of the NIST Director's strategic priorities: to foster more efficient transactions in the domestic and global marketplace through development and use of effective standards by manufacturing and service sectors.

NIST has a long tradition of standards development. The Administration's American Competitiveness Initiative of 2006, for example, highlights NIST's role in supporting the development of standards used by the public and private sectors. NIST participation includes:
- carrying out research that provides the technical underpinning for standards;
- participating in standards development activities in a broad range of technical areas;
- providing technical information related to standards;
- participating extensively in international industrial consortia; and
- in some cases, providing calibrations and standard reference materials (SRMs) called for in the standards.

Congress has given NIST additional standards-related responsibilities in several specific areas of current national interest, including: IT security, biometrics and voting. In particular, under the National Technology Transfer and Advancement Act (NTTAA) of 1996, Congress has charged NIST to coordinate standards activities among Federal agencies and with State and local governments for the purpose of promoting participation in private sector voluntary standards activities and making greater use of available voluntary standards rather than relying or depending on developing in-house standards.

Our objective is to have a capability that provides 1) a comprehensive picture of NIST's documentary standards development activities and 2) the ability to assess their impact. There are many choices of standards venues with which to participate. NIST's participation is broad, but selective. Our ultimate goal is to be able to provide advice to the stakeholder community inside and outside NIST on the best use of the resources dedicated to documentary standards development.

One of NIST's strategic priorities is to develop and encourage the use of effective standards by the manufacturing and service sectors. There is ample evidence that standards foster, and indeed are integral to, economic growth and development, and that the role of standards-related activities is increasingly important to international competitiveness in technology-based markets. Conceptually, we understand the role of all these infratechnologies in the design, development, production, and marketing of products and services.[3] NIST has an important role in supporting the development, diffusion, and impact of physical standards and measurement technologies.

---

[1] This is a follow-up study to NISTIR 7398 "Selected Impacts of Documentary Standards Supported by NIST" and part of a broader Technology Services (TS) effort to assess the impact of documentary standards on global competitiveness and innovation.

There are grounds for asserting that documentary standards are an important factor in reducing risks and transactions costs in product and service markets. Recent studies, as well, indicate that documentary standards are correlated with indicators of economic growth at the macroeconomic level.[4] However, public and private organizations in the United States and globally lack a well-developed understanding of the role, nature and impact of documentary standards.[5] This unawareness complicates NIST's ability to inform its own leadership and other stakeholders of the best ways to manage this critical responsibility.

Several people supported the work reflected in this report, with special credit to David Leech[6] for work on success stories and impact analysis guidance, and Joanne Henson,[7] who assisted with the early data analysis.

III. Proposed Approach

This report highlights NIST's effort to fill this "awareness vacuum" by providing a strategic assessment of the role and impact of NIST's documentary standards efforts. The initial canvassing study identified 55 high impact standards projects and described some of their characteristics[8] Figure 3 describes the three stages of Technology Services' proposed approach.[9]

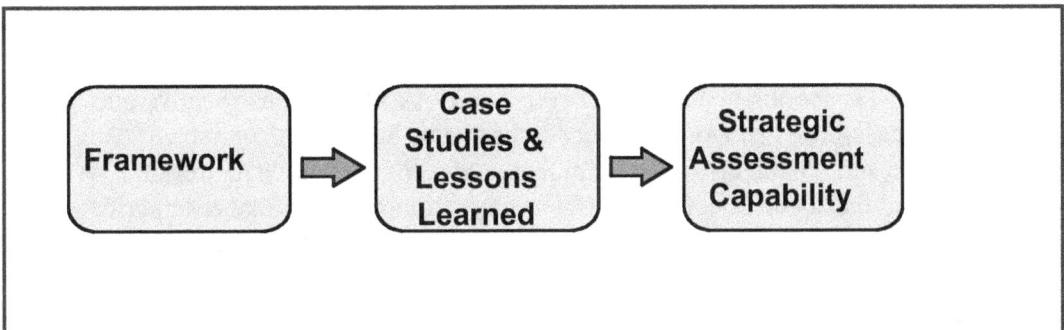

Figure 3. Strategic Assessment Development Process

Technology Services' canvassing efforts are part of the first stage of this process. The near-term goal is to describe NIST's documentary standards activities and to begin the iterative process of constructing a conceptual *framework* for talking about, communicating, and exploring the nature and impact of these efforts. This includes questions such as the following:

- What "kinds" of documentary standards can we distinguish in the information we have gathered?
- What is the extent of NIST's participation in the various "kinds" of documentary standards development efforts?
- What other types of organizations are involved in the development of

documentary standards?
- What is the extent of other organizations' involvement?
- Over and above the formal distinctions between types of standards activities, do NIST's activities cluster along dimensions that might make them distinguishable in terms of high, medium, and low potential impact?
- Are they distinguishable in terms of underlying technologies, or industries served, or in terms of their national or international scope?
- What are the obvious, near-term consequences (outcomes) of these efforts?

As a conceptual *framework* for NIST's documentary standards activity begins to emerge, it will be compared with, and possibly integrated with, other more general, frameworks that that have been developed to describe NIST's overall role in the nation's (indeed, the world's) technical measurement and economic systems.[10] Integrating NIST's documentary standards activities into these more general frameworks is important in the transition to the second, *case studies & lessons learned*, step in our approach.

In the ***case studies & lessons learned step*** we will ask a different set of questions than asked in the first step. How do we understand the impact of NIST's documentary standards development activity? The two obvious answers — technical impact and economic impact — are related, but it is often harder to discern economic impact. During the second step of the proposed process, the relationships among the components (variables) of our emerging framework are hypothesized and associated with outcomes. Case studies are designed to test these associations.[11]

The broad outlines of this phase are already in view, thanks to the past and ongoing efforts of NIST's economic assessment community. A host of retrospective and prospective case-based economic impact assessments have been conducted.[12] On the basis of these and related efforts, we can formulate a conservative model for understanding the social benefits of NIST's interaction with voluntary standards organizations. A company invests resources in voluntary standards development activities (often in the form of in-kind labor time contributions) up to the point where the expected value of additional resources invested (for example, another hour of in-kind labor time) equals the present discounted value (or present value) of the additional expected benefits (from the additional investment) to the company. Investment up to the point where the marginal benefit for the company equals its marginal cost will maximize the net present value of its investment.[13] The present value of the company's investments will thus be a lower bound on the expected present value of the company's benefits from those investments. Moreover, the sum of the discounted individual company benefits would be a lower bound estimate of the expected social benefits of the voluntary standards development process because some of the benefits will spill over to other companies and to consumers. It is reasonable to postulate that these social benefits will be higher where NIST provides specialized cost-effective resources to the voluntary standards development process.

Candidate impact studies are already emerging from the canvassing process (78 high impact standards identified) as participants describe 1) their level of involvement, 2) the identity of private and other public sector participants and their level of involvement, 3) the outputs from these activities, and 4) an estimate of any change in scope or timing of the documentary standards activity due to NIST's involvement. In the future as case study impact assessments are selected and performed, a thorough understanding of the nature of NIST's activities will begin to emerge and our understanding of how, and under what circumstances, significant economic impacts come to fruition. Accumulations of these case-based explanations are valuable as internal "lessons learned." They are also valuable as a potent means of communicating NIST's role to stakeholders about NIST's important contributions to the nation's national innovation system.

Over time, as we accumulate knowledge of high impact activities and those of lesser impact, and we clarify the circumstances in which these outcomes transpire, we will move into ***step three of our strategic assessment development process.*** We will begin to:

- formulate, test, and periodically verify the types of activities NIST does best;
- offer advice about where documentary standards resources should be focused for greatest impact; and
- identify NIST's optimal role in these activities.

We will begin to answer the following types of questions:

- What can be done to create more effective and efficient standards development processes?
- Where is NIST concentrating its efforts today?
- Where should NIST be concentrating for the future?
- On what basis is such a strategy established? Is the nature of documentary standards development changing?
- Is the pace of these developments changing?
- Is NIST facilitating strategic change?
- Are these changes productive?

In time, we envision that our efforts at developing, testing, and improving strategic assessment criteria will evolve into an ongoing "*indicators*" approach that will allow managers to "take the pulse" of ongoing documentary standards activities. For example, it could turn out that when NIST personnel from multiple operating units are engaged in creating a cluster of related standards, those standards tend to have greater impact individually and collectively. Or, it could be that when the ratio of industry participants to NIST participants is exceptionally high, the resulting standards tend to have high impact. To the extent that such factors can be confidently demonstrated to "lead" the emergence of high impact documentary standards activities, they could be construed as "leading indicators" of effective standards activities and, more importantly, serve as guidelines for future activities.

In summary, Technology Services has launched a long-term effort to assess the extent, nature, and outcomes of NIST's involvement in documentary standards development activities. The initial and on-going canvassing activities (this paper) are part of a three-step approach to thoroughly understand NIST's role in these activities and the impact.

The long-term goal is to develop an assessment capability and integrate it into NIST's planning, evaluation, and resource allocation cycle. The ultimate objective is to improve the standards development process to help promote U.S. innovation and industrial competitiveness.

IV. Report Methodology

The data in Table 1 were used to direct the search for specific standards development activities where NIST's participation might have produced significant, positive impacts. Emphasis was placed on identifying standards efforts that were fairly recent and that resulted in (or were expected to result in) either broad adoption of the standard or significant economic or social impact. The intent was to limit the collection of information to a handful of successful documentary standards efforts and to use this information as a basis for choosing activities to be the subject of future retrospective case studies.

The results from the first canvassing study (NISTIR 7398) were sent to all NIST OU's in late 2007 requesting updates to the initial set of 55 projects or additions to the original list. In addition, the following "potential impact" questions were included:

Participation
1. *Estimate the number of hours (of NIST personnel) dedicated to the development of a given standard.*
2. *Estimate the multiple of total NIST hours that non-NIST participants dedicated to the development of this documentary standard.*
3. *Were any industry consortia involved in the development of this standard?*

Output
4. *In the absence of NIST's participation in the development of this documentary standard, would the scope of the resulting standard be broader, narrower, or about the same? Is there any evidence you could cite to support this claim?*
5. *Did NIST personnel publish any professional papers as a result of their participation in the development of this documentary standard?*

Effect
6. *If everything about this documentary standard development effort remained the same except for NIST participation, estimate when the standard would have been published.*
7. *What products or services are available, or available at a lower cost, or available more broadly, or available in different qualities, or available earlier that would not be available in the absence of this standard?*

After reviewing the results, more in-depth information was sought on three projects where the impact rationale was well articulated and plausible and where it was judged that a short "success story" would be relatively easy to develop. The success stories are also referred to as "descriptive case studies" which examine what happened, describe the context in which it happened, explore how and why, and. consider what would have happened otherwise. Thus case study can be particularly useful in the exploratory phases of a program such as this effort by Technology Services.[14] We contacted pertinent staff and stakeholders to gather additional information or clarify results by asking follow-up questions and discussing results. The success stories help to fill the "awareness vacuum" by providing a more detailed look at the need for a new standard, the research that was required, NIST's specific role and contributions, and the resulting success, including a description of the impact. These are presented in section VI.

V. NIST Participation

In understanding NIST's commitment to the development of high quality standards, it is useful to know where and how many NIST staff members participate in the activities of key standards development organizations (SDOs). Staff participate on committees where their technical competence matches committee needs and where they can ensure that US. national interests are represented. NIST's commitment of resources to the development of documentary standards is substantial. The Standards Committee Participation (SCP) database, which attempts to capture all NIST participation in the committees of SDOs and consortia, shows over 400 NIST staff members involved in the development of documentary standards. Table 1 displays the number of NIST staff members, organized by NIST OU, participating in the standards activities of the listed SDOs as of August 2008.

Table 1. NIST Participation in Standards Committees by OU

OU	No. of Staff Members	Committee Memberships	No. SDOs	Top SDO's (# membership)
Office of the Director	7	10	5	HPS (4) ASTM (3) ANSI (1)[2]
Technology Services	32	195	21	OIML (51) ASTM (43) ANSI (25)
Technology Innovation Program	2	2	2	ASTM(1) OLA (1)
Center for Neutron Research	4	13	3	ANS (8) ISO (4)
Center for Nanoscale Science and Technology	2	7	4	ISO (3) ASME (2)
Electronics and Electrical Engineering Laboratory	47	145	19	ASTM (28) IEC (28) IEEE (26)
Manufacturing Engineering Laboratory	52	185	28	ASME (43) ISO (26) ASA (16)
Chemical Science and Technology Laboratory	65	189	30	ASTM (89) CIPM (15) ISO (15)
Physics Laboratory	45	201	26	ASTM (48) IEEE (28) CIPM (23) CIE (23)
Materials Science and Engineering Laboratory	33	128	10	ASTM (87) ISO (17) ADA (13)
Building and Fire Research Laboratory	49	177	18	ASTM (79) NFPA (23) ACI (22)
Information Technology Laboratory	66	146	25	INCITS (35) IETF (22) NIST (14)
Totals	**404**	**1398**		

---

[2] ANSI is not an SDO, but coordinates the development and use of voluntary consensus standards in the United States and represents the needs and views of U.S. stakeholders in standardization forums around the globe. NIST staff chair or participate in a broad range of ANSI policy committee activities. In addition, some of the activities counted as "ANSI" activities reflect NIST staff participation in ANSI-accredited standards committees, which are administered by other SDOs.

NIST provides technical leadership in standards development in a number of technology areas. NIST also works closely with industry to translate NIST research results into appropriate standards. A common theme of the standards efforts documented in Table 3 was NIST support for testing and other conformity assessment activities associated with the standards. Other NIST contributions included: conducting research that formed the basis of the standard; working cooperatively with industry to establish appropriate requirements; and developing applicable software.

VI. Findings

The results of the canvassing identified 78 documentary standards efforts that are considered to have significant impact, or that are widely used and adopted. This is an increase of 23 projects (or 42%) from the first canvassing study published in early 2007. Table 2 contains a sample from each OU to illustrate the wide variety and the broad scope of the impacts and the resulting public benefits. It is important to note that the impact/benefits noted in the table were self-reported by the participants. In only a few cases were the impacts/benefits based on quantitative data or previous study results. The complete results are presented in Table 5, which due to its length is included at the end of the report.

Table 2. Sample Overview of Impacts Derived from NIST -Supported Standards Efforts

Lab	Title	Description & NIST Roles	Impact	SDO
BFRL	Sustainable Building	In developing its Building for Environmental and Economic Sustainability (BEES) tool, NIST applied standards for life cycle assessment, life cycle costing, multiattribute decision analysis, and building element classification. Once BEES was published, NIST wrote initial draft of biobased product sustainability assessment standard.	▪ More than 24,000 users rely on BEES software for building products. ▪ BEES also being applied to biobased products as required by federal regulation implementing Section 9002 of the 2002 Farm Bill	ASTM SP D7075 (Evaluating and Reporting Environmental Performance of Biobased Products), ISO
CSTL	Alternative Refrigerants	NIST engaged in research that would allow industry to make the switch to alternative refrigerants in a timely and economic fashion to meet the timetable imposed by the Montreal Protocol of 1987 to develop alternatives to CFCs. NIST researchers developed the REFPROP database which contains precompetitive properties data so that industry could design their own proprietary CFC alternatives. ISO has incorporated this into their standard.	▪ A comparison of industry benefits with the funding stream of NIST's research program estimated a social rate of return of at least 433% and a BC ratio of 4 to 1 (1998 study).	ISO (2004)

EEEL	Restriction of Certain Hazardous Substances in Electronic Products (ROHS)	NIST was instrumental in facilitating the development of a Materials Declaration Management standard (consisting of UML model, XML schema and 2 interactive PDF forms) necessary for U.S. companies to show compliance with an EU directive, which bans electrical products exceeding the specified threshold amounts for 6 hazardous substances used in electronics.	▪ Any company that sells an electrical product in EU member nations after 7/1/06 must declare the hazardous content information. ▪ NIST work is assisting U.S. industry to stay competitive in Europe, and has promoted information exchange between large and small firms.	IPC (2006) (also iNEMI)
ITL	Digital Encryption Standard (DES) and Advanced Encryption Standard (AES)	NIST developed DES standard to support electronic transactions and implemented conformance testing. In 1997, NIST announced initiation of the effort to replace DES with a new advanced encryption module, which implements symmetric key cryptography. Implemented as FIPS standards in 2001.	▪ DES was critical in launching the commercial encryption industry. ▪ Users realized significant operational efficiencies ▪ DES was critical to rise of electronic banking. ▪ Since introduction of AES, approximately 200 AES products have been approved.	FIPS 46 (1977) 46-3 (1999) 197 (2001)
MEL	Quality Measurement Data (QMD)	The QMD spec is the work of the MEPT Quality Measurement (MEQM) working group of the Automotive Industry Action Group (AIAG) Metrology Project Team (MEPT). The goal of the MEQM has been to produce a non-proprietary, computer-readable, and widely implemented standard for the interface between measurement devices (not merely dimensional) and Statistical Process Control (SPC) analysis software packages.	▪ The QMD standard holds promise to save statistical process control (SPC) software industry in the U.S. alone around $50 million over the next few years. This estimate is based on verifiable data from reliable sources.	AIAG
MSEL	Hardness Standardization for Metals	NIST was instrumental in the research to establish a traceability system for hardness measurements, developing SRMs and is refining test methods. NIST has most accurate hardness machine in the U.S.	▪ Huge impact on trade of metals. Establishes national chain of traceability to fundamental SI units. ▪ Disputes between producers and users curtailed. ▪ Information gained from NIST's participation in the CIPM has influenced ASTM requirements.	ASTM, ISO (1991-2007)
PL	Specifications for the Chromaticity of Solid State Lighting Products	NIST led the development of this standard (ANSI C38.377), which is under final approval. This standard specifies the white light chromaticity ranges for solid state lighting (SSL) products. This standard will ensure that new lighting products using LEDs will have high-quality white light and appropriately classified according to color temperature to allow smooth replacement of traditional light sources or other SSL products having similar color.	▪ DOE is starting the Energy Star program for SSL products, which needs this standard. ▪ All SSL products should be designed to meet this standard, and in turn, white LEDs (used for the SSL products) will also be deigned and classified for color according to this standard. ▪ This standard will have significant impact on both white LED and SSL industries.	ANSI

The cited projects cut across all laboratories and reflect diverse technical areas and applications. Based on an analysis of these projects, eight categories were specifically identified with the remainder grouped into 'Other'. The results are displayed in Table 3.

Table 3. Application Areas

Category	Count
Safety	13
Homeland Security	9
Environment	4
Energy Efficiency	8
Health	5
Information Tech.	10
Supply Chain	10
Measurement Science	14
Other	5
Total	*78*

Also, 24 of the 78 projects (31%) fit broadly under one of the 14 NIST budget initiatives for FY 2009[15]. Some can be categorized as falling under one of NIST's previous programmatic Strategic Focus Areas. This type of information could be useful in better focusing NIST standards development work in the future.

An additional observation is that 28 of the identified standards were adopted or developed by the three major international standards organizations (ISO/IEC/ITU). Based on SDO membership reported by NIST staff listed in Table 1, this figure is somewhat higher than would be expected. It may indicate that many of the standards efforts that were considered to have had a significant impact by the NIST OUs required broad, international cooperation where national participation is a priority. This is valued by industry-specific sectors and helps ensure that U.S. companies maintain their competitive advantage in the national and international market place. In the remaining 51 cases, NIST involvement focused on supporting U.S.-based standards developing organizations or consortia, most of whose standards and specifications are used globally. (see Figure 4).

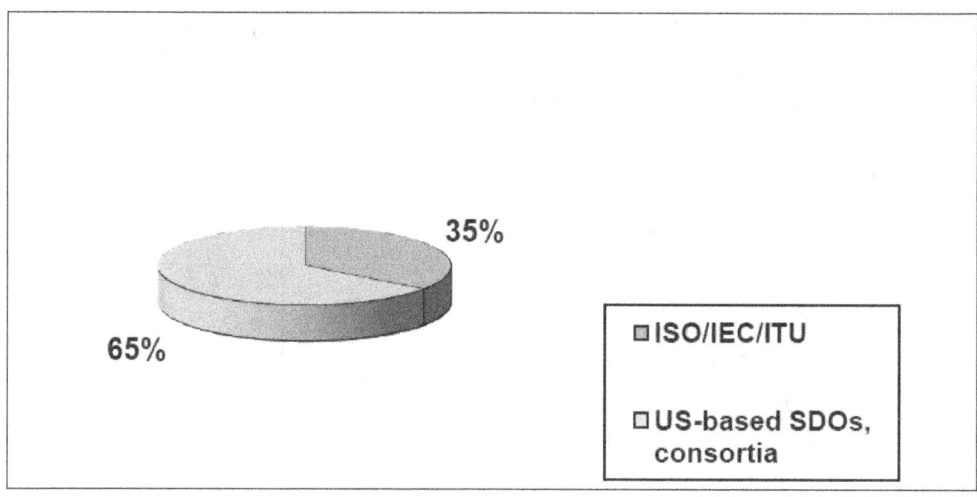

Figure 4: Breakdown of Standards Participation by Organization Type

VII. Reported Outcomes

As part of this second phase of NIST's standards canvassing effort, seven (7) additional questions were posed to the OUs about the projects identified in the first and second rounds of canvassing. These seven questions attempt to capture evidence of outcomes from NIST's participation in voluntary standards development activity. Table 4 describes the additional information requested and the rationale for the outcomes.

Table 4. Description of Intermediate Outcome Metrics

Additional Data Area Item	Impact Rationale
Non-NIST labor time	The time that industry devotes to the development of a documentary standard is a lower bound estimate of the cumulative (social) value of the standard to industry.
NIST labor time	The ratio non-NIST labor time to NIST labor time is a gross indicator of a lower bound net outcome from a documentary standards project. The greater the ratio the greater the potential leveraging effect of NIST's labor time investment.
Standard scope w/o NIST participation	Because NIST participation frequently supports the grounding of standards on measurement science, the scope of standards can apply to more products or services.

Standard timing w/o NIST participation	Because NIST is frequently perceived as an "honest broker," the time required to negotiate consensus among industry participants is reduced (resulting in lower transaction costs) and standards are implemented sooner than they would be otherwise.
Publications resulting from NIST participation	These publications are project outputs. If publications can be linked to indicators of economic value, such as highly cited patents, these can be claimed as secondary evidence of economic benefits.[3]
New or improved product/service availability	Some fraction of the value added from new product/service availability can be claimed as a benefit of NISTs standards development activity.[16]
Industry group/consortium participation	Participation in industry consortia is linked to improvements in productivity and profitability.[4]

Responses were received for 53 of the 78 projects (68%). Not all of them were complete, but some interesting observations begin to shed light on the impact of NIST's involvement with the standards development process.

- Observation: The average multiple of non-NIST hours to NIST hours for all 53 projects answering the questions was 11.77.

    o Implication: This means that, on average, for every full-time-equivalent of NIST staff working on one of the high impact standards, almost 12 times that amount of non-NIST staff (primarily industry) were supporting the project. This suggests that NIST leverages valuable industry labor, and is indicative of the lower bound estimate of the social benefits of standards development activities.

- Observation: Of 21 projects that answered the question regarding when the standard would have been published without NIST participation, the average was 1.65 years later.

    o Implication: This gap is an intermediate indicator of NISTs unique contributions from an economic perspective. It is a gross indicator of the transaction time savings that NIST involvement in a voluntary standards development effort affords industry.

---

[3] A. Jaffee and M. Trajtenberg, *Patents, Citations, and Innovations,* MIT Press, 2002.
[4] A. Link and D. Siegel, *Technological Change and Economic Performance,* Routledge, 2003, pp. 111-114.

- Observation: Of the 53 respondents, approximately one-third (34 percent) indicated that the scope of the standard would have been narrower without NIST involvement.

    - Implication: Increased standard breadth is another intermediate indicator of the unique contribution that NIST involvement in a voluntary standards development effort affords industry. It is a gross indicator of an increase in the number of newly available products or services enabled by the standard in question. Combined with time saving due to NIST's participation, the increase in scope scales up the economic benefits that flow from NIST's participation in voluntary standards development efforts.[17]

- Observation: Of the 53 projects, 62% had involvement from industry groups or consortia in developing the standard.

    - Implication: This percentage is indicative of strong industry support and, ultimately, significant economic impact. If, as anticipated, the economic impact of NIST's involvement in documentary standards development efforts is highest when industry is most committed, and when NIST brings specialized and cost-effective resources to the effort, the involvement of industry groups, and especially of consortia (which usually are structured to achieve specific ends on the basis of the specialized resource contributions of members) are an early indicator of significant benefits.[18]

- Observation: Forty-two (42) percent of respondents stated that the standard resulted in having a product or service available, or available at a lower cost, or available more broadly, or available in different qualities, or available earlier that would not be in the absence of the standard. In addition, many of the other respondents who did not specifically claim new products or services did claim broader societal benefits such as: trade facilitation, increased homeland security, interoperability benefits, etc.

    - Implication: Standards provide tangible results that could benefit from more precise characterization.

- Observation: Finally, as may be expected, a large majority (85 percent) of the projects resulted in professional publications, including journal articles, conference proceedings and presentations, NIST publications, magazine articles and other reports.

    - Implication: These publications are a non-economic indicator of the secondary output of NIST's engagement with voluntary standards organizations.

We also analyzed two sub-sets of the data, looking at those projects which resulted in new or improved products or services, as well as all those projects which had industry group or consortia involvement to see if these two subsets had any differentiating characteristics.

- Observation: Taking a look at only those 23 projects that have reported claims that the standard has had an impact on actual products and services finds a higher ratio of non-NIST participants to NIST staff (15.3 v 11.8).

    o Implication: This indicates a higher rate of external (likely industry) participation.

- Observation: These same 23 projects also reflect a very high rate of industry association/consortia involvement of 91 percent.

    o Implication: This compares to 62 percent for the entire sample of 53 projects. Therefore, higher industry involvement in standards development is likely an indicator of greater focus on commercialization.

- Observation: The second group of 33 projects which claimed the participation of industry associations or consortia also yielded some interesting, but not unexpected, findings. For all these projects, 58 percent claimed new/improved products or services, as opposed to 42 percent of the entire sample.

Taken together, it is clear that many of these NIST standards projects leveraged the work of non-NIST participants and the participation of industry groups to develop high impact standards that were developed on average 1.5 years earlier and resulted in product and service improvements, general benefits to the country and a large number of publications and presentations. If we look at the subsets, industry involvement is, as expected, associated with a larger percentage of new or improved products/services. No attempt has been made yet to put an economic value on the resulting goods and services or the faster development time.

NIST involvement in voluntary standards development efforts need not result in new products or services to generate significant economic impacts. The only basic prerequisite is that NIST bring valuable resources to a process that is also of value to the marketplace of producers and consumers. Where new products and services are available, additional benefit streams will have been induced. Where NIST contributed uniquely to the flow of those benefits, the returns to NIST's resources investments, specifically, will be higher yet.[19]

Each of the three following "Success Stories" begins to place these outcome indicators in context and to gather some more detailed information on how NIST's involvement contributed to the overall success of the standard development activity in question.

VIII. 16 CFR Part 1633 Standard for the Flammability (Open Flame) of Mattress Sets

Executive Summary

In the late 1990's and early 2000's, industry and public concern about loss of life from bedroom fires motivated a hard look at ways to reduce deaths and property damage. Participants struggling to resolve issues knew standards were part of the solution, but could not agree on ways to establish, test and codify standards. NIST, known as objective and technically proficient, got the call to engage with industry and regulators to help create standards that would be effective, but not onerous. Figure 1 is a thumbnail of the process, going from the need for new standards, to the research conducted by NIST, which led to a successful regulation. This report highlights the process and explains many of the benefits that resulted from NIST's work.

Background

From 1999 to 2002 about 15,300 fires occurred annually where the first item ignited was a mattress and its bedding. These fires resulted in an annual average of 350 deaths, 1,750 injuries, 295 million dollars in property loss, and untold human suffering.[5] In June of 2007, the U.S. Consumer Product Safety Commission (CPSC) announced the implementation of a new product safety standard for mattresses. Mattresses manufactured on or after July 1, 2007 must meet the U.S. Consumer Product Safety Commission's (CPSC) flammability standard, known as 16 CFR Part 1633. The mandatory standard is designed to reduce the severity of mattress fires ignited by open flame sources such as candles, matches and lighters. Figure 2 shows a pre-standard bed ignited by a match-size flame; within 5 minutes the entire bed can be fully involved.

Working with the International Sleep Products Association (ISPA) and its research affiliate, the Sleep Products Safety Council (SPSC) through a special Cooperative Research and Development Agreement (CRADA), NIST's Building and Fire Research Laboratory (BFRL) developed the scientific basis for CPSC's mattress flammability standard.[6]

The CPSC estimates that the 1633 standard will prevent as many as 270 deaths and 1,330 injuries every year. Without NIST's involvement, many of these lives would not be saved and many of these injuries and property losses would not be prevented. But over and above such immediate and obvious benefits, it seems clear that without NIST's technical support the mattress industry would have suffered significant economic losses by adopting a less substantiated standard. The cost of these mattress industry related losses in California alone, was estimated in 2002 to be

---

[5] David Miller, *Mattress and Bedding Fire Loss Estimates for 1999-2000*, USCPSC, 2005, cited in, Soumaya Tohamy, *Final Regulatory Analysis of Staff's Draft Final Standard to Address Open-Flame Ignitions of Mattress Sets*, Directorate of Economic Analysis, USCPSC, January 10, 2006.

[6] ISPA and SPSC together account for more than 700 wholesalers, retailers, and manufacturers of mattresses and mattress foundations. Their members account for 80 percent of total U.S. sales of mattresses and mattress sets.

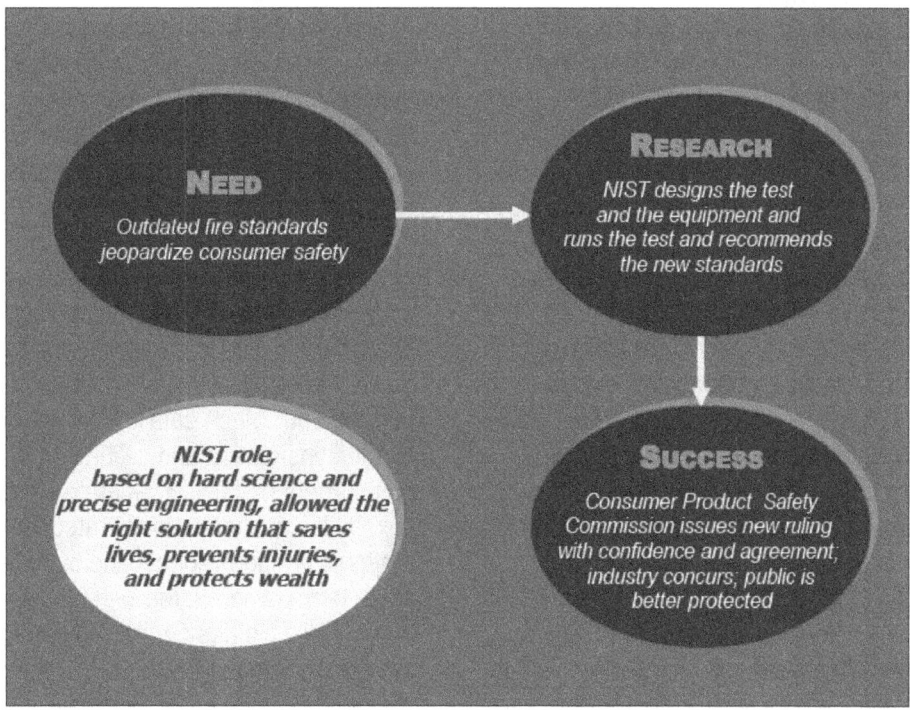

Figure 1F: NIST involvement in standards development directly affects public safety

approximately $276 million less in mattress sales and $15 million less in California state tax revenues. Since these losses reflect the difference between adopting the standard that was underwritten by NIST and adopting what industry argued was a less appropriate standard put forward by the California's Bureau of Home Furnishings & Thermal Insulation (hereafter, "the California Bureau"), these potential net losses can be construed as part of the indirect economic benefits that flow to society from NIST's efforts.

Origin of the effort

The mattresses that U.S. consumers purchase must comply with fire safety regulations. In particular, since the 1970s mattress manufacturers have had to ensure that the materials from which their products were made do not readily ignite from dropped cigarettes, as codified in 16 CFR Part 1632. Industry efficiently implemented this standard nationwide and consistent industry compliance contributed significantly to a substantial reduction over the past 25 years in residential fire deaths.

In 2000, the Consumer Product Safety Commission received a petition to modify the current flammability standard to include sources of ignition other than cigarettes. The Commission initiated a proceeding to develop a mandatory federal standard to address open-flame ignitions in 2001 and published a proposed regulation in January 2005. Accordingly, a mattress manufacturer would test three mattress sets of the same prototype mattress set and pass technical criteria pertaining to the rate and total amount of heat a burning mattress releases in the first 10 minutes after ignition and the peak rate at which it releases heat for 30 minutes after mattress ignition. Since the first item typically ignited is bedclothes (sheets, etc.), the ignition source intended here must mimic burning bedclothes.

The fire resistance standards proposed by the California Bureau in its Technical Bulletin 603 would have required that a mattress and box spring combination be fire resistant when exposed to a particular open flame source. To qualify as a safe mattress under the California Bureau's criteria, a mattress and box spring had to burn at a low level (maximum instantaneous heat release rate of 150 kilowatts) for at least 60 minutes. The California Bureau intended to finalize its regulations in November 2003 and to require that all mattresses and box springs manufactured for sale in California beginning January 1, 2004 meet these standards. A major source of uncertainty here was that the California Bureau's flame source bore no known relation to burning bedclothes.

NIST gets involved

Part of NIST's core mission is to pursue research and develop technology that pertains to measurement: how long, how fast, how heavy, how hot, how accurate, how precise? Another NIST core mission is to support the development of U.S. industry's voluntary standards development activities. NIST's support of the CPSC's mattress regulation brings together these core mission areas.

The Sleep Products Safety Council (SPSC) initiated a CRADA with the Building and Fire Research Laboratory of NIST in response to a published notice from CPSC that they planned to investigate the possible need for a regulation in this area. NIST's involvement began in 1998 and continued until the regulation was imposed in July, 2007 on all new residential mattresses sold in the U. S. NIST developed the only science-based approach to the issue of mattress flammability, looking at the problem from beginning to end. Initial research was directed at a viable test method for simulating the damage that flaming bedclothes (sheets, blankets, etc.) inflict on a mattress. This required the development of a new technique for measuring the highly transient and spatially erratic heat fluxes that burning bedclothes entail. This was followed by the construction and calibration of a set of gas burners that could generate similar heat fluxes. It was then demonstrated that mattress fire behavior caused by exposure to these burners correlated with that seen with burning bed clothes on the same mattress. The final portion of the work focused on development of a basis for predicting what various levels of improved mattress fire performance implied in terms of potential lives saved per year. This gave a rational basis for the peak fire size that a regulator might allow from a mattress when tested with the gas burners (and a guideline for a cost-benefit analysis of any regulation).

The research conducted by NIST showed that the peak heat release rate proposed by the California Bureau was unnecessarily low, and the duration of the test longer than necessary. In addition, as noted, their ignition conditions bore an unclear relation to the hazard. The risk of bedroom flash-over can be minimized if mattress, box spring, and bedclothes fire does not exceed 400 kilowatts. The California Bureau's proposed heat release rate of 150 kilowatts would have required much higher product design costs, but the products would not have been more effective in preventing flash-over. The 60-minute test duration proposed by the California Bureau was regarded as both impractical (the vast majority of mattress producers could not make commercially-viable product under California's proposed rule) and ultimately counterproductive (as higher priced mattresses would significantly reduce the number of safe mattresses sold). Lab tests showed that when ignited some pre-standard bed ensembles proceed to flash-over conditions in the room of origin (invariably fatal to room residents and highly threatening to other home occupants) within five minutes. The typical time for a fire department to respond to a residential call is five to nine minutes, according to the National Fire Protection Association (NFPA). Avoiding flash-over within the first ten to twenty minutes post-ignition would significantly improve life safety by allowing sufficient time for escape and rescue.

Figure 2F: Burning Bed at One and a Half Minutes

What would have been done, absent NIST?

If NIST had not participated, CPSC might have gone forward on the basis of its own limited resources. Presumably, it would have taken CPSC longer to develop an alternative to the criteria proposed by the California Bureau. Strong industry resistance to the imposition of such a standard can also be a "show stopper." Under this scenario, the lives lost, as well as the injuries and property loses that would have occurred in the intervening time gap can be interpreted as benefits unique to NIST's involvement. As an alternative to "new CPSC standard" scenario, we might well imagine industry-sponsored efforts to modify the existing California public occupancy standard (Technical Bulletin 603).

It is unlikely that either of these two paths would have produced a test method that was based on an in-depth analysis of the problem since neither organization has the resources (money or trained staff) to do this. Furthermore, the mattress industry is not an R&D intensive industry so it seems unlikely that a science-based consensus standard would have emerged. It is likely that a standard might have emerged after a few years whose potential effectiveness at solving the real world problem could not really be assessed. It seems certain that they would have gone no further than the methodology devised by NIST. They might have "gotten to market" sooner (since the TB 603 test already existed) but the effectiveness of that test would be unclear.

Compared to the NIST fire science based approach, the alternative approach made it very difficult to know if expensive compliance would translate into real world improvements in life safety. In such situations industry resistance can prevent the development of important safety standards and regulations, resulting in continued losses and injuries.

Conclusion

NIST's support in providing a factual foundation and rationale for the desired performance level in the standard represented a superior outcome to the proposed alternative standard and prevented a costly delay in implementing a standard nationwide. NIST's deep and unique experience with measurement technology provides a sure foundation for mattress safety and as a result consumers are safer.

IX. Development of Radiation Detector Standards for Homeland Security Applications

Executive Summary

Since 9/11, one of the most frightening threats that has disrupted many a night's sleep were "dirty bombs," explosives salted with radiological materials and smuggled through an American port. It was feared that a single dirty bomb attack could cost billions, kill hundreds, and take years of recovery.

The chaos of 9/11 quickly turned into widespread resolve to better protect U.S. citizens. The challenge faced was simple and profoundly daunting: create and deploy rugged detector equipment that could be used easily by non-specialists and first responders to scan massive amounts of cargo for nuclear-radiological threats.

Speed and precision were driving factors for the diverse group that coalesced to confront this challenge. DHS pressed hard on the group, urging them to "fast-track" detection equipment and training standards. Leadership quickly fell to NIST, with its wide and deep experience in creating, testing, and validating standards. NIST chaired the "N42 Committee" that coordinated and integrated the work of several diverse groups, addressing radioactivity measurements, homeland security, and protection instrumentation.

NIST guided the dedicated and highly proficient groups to create the technical foundation for a suite of standards that reflected the complexities of the challenges presented by equipment from small, hand-held detectors to massive, port-screening monitors, including standard data formats to easily process readouts. These groups also designed the training essential to move the standards from the working groups to effective field protection practices. The initial effort took two years of intense work during 2002-2004.

The operational experiences that followed pointed to even more effective protocols, and NIST engaged in another two more years of concentrated proceedings refining the standards. Today, users and vendors have access to a set of nine specific standards for radiation detection, which cover instrumentation, alarms, and fixed and mobile systems, easing the burdens on industry and defenders

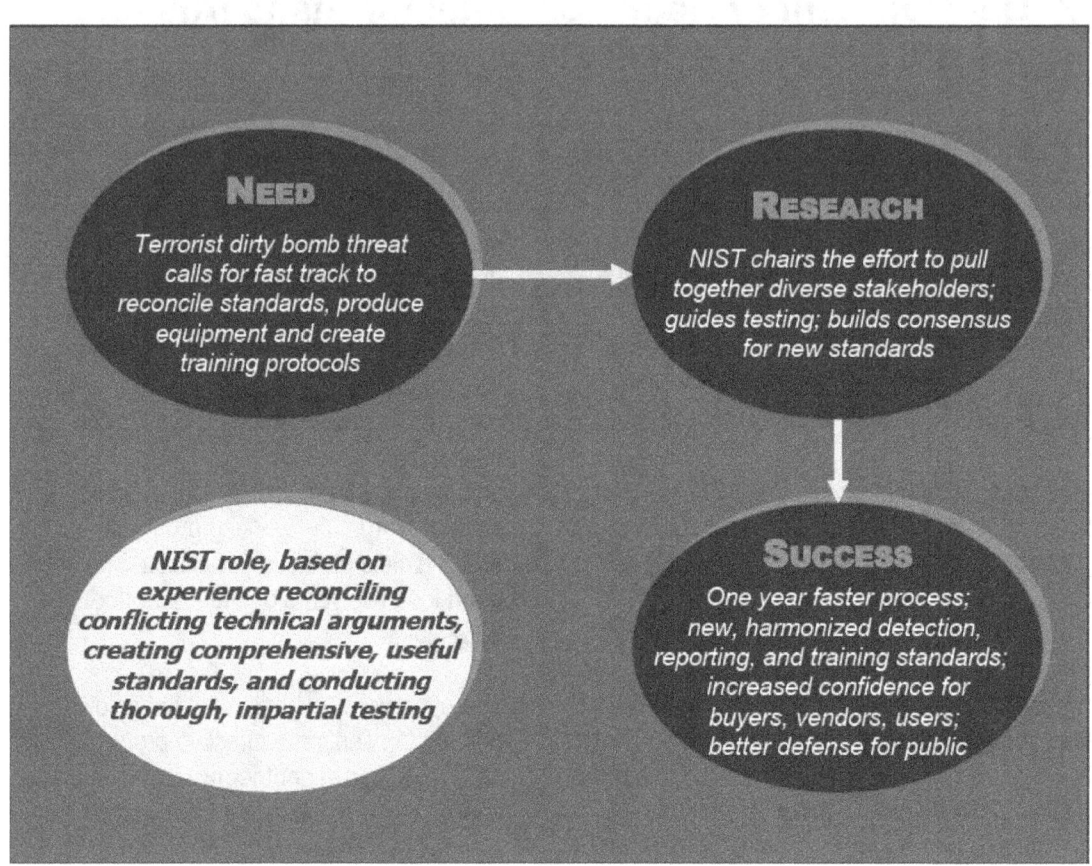

Figure 1R: NIST technical leadership contributes to protection of U.S. citizens and property

Introduction

In collaboration with the U.S. Department of Homeland Security (DHS), industry, and other national laboratories, the National Institute of Standards and Technology (NIST) responded to the nation's needs for increased port security in the post-9/11 environment. On DHS's behalf, NIST radiation experts took part in and led an effort to fast-track a suite of radiation detection standards through the voluntary consensus standard process. These standards set performance requirements for radiation detection equipment based on homeland security needs, and will increase the effectiveness and efficiency of cargo, vehicle, and other screening processes and reduce the risks of dramatic terrorist attacks on U.S. soil.

In one of the DHS planning scenarios, high explosives, radioactive sources, and other "dirty bomb" components are smuggled into the country in sea-land containers shipped to U.S. ports under assumed business names. The containers are picked up and transferred to safe houses near three target cities. After detonation, thirty-six blocks are contaminated by the initial explosion and the spread of radioactive contamination by mild winds. The scenario estimates several hundred fatalities and injuries, extensive environmental contamination, and the evacuation of thousands of individuals in each city. Bus, rail, and air transport routes are altered, and highway checkpoints are established to monitor incoming traffic for contamination. Hospitals in each region, already at maximum capacity with injuries from the blasts, are inundated with up to 50,000 "worried well." Sewage treatment plants are quickly contaminated; businesses are closed for an extended duration while radioactive contamination is remediated; and local tax revenues plummet. The entire contaminated area is economically depressed for years. The total economic impact is in the billions of dollars.7

With scenarios like this in mind after 9-11, efforts to screen the vast amount of cargo that floods into U.S. ports increased dramatically. While some of the equipment needed to monitor cargo arriving by vehicles and vessels had been available previously, it was not available in the ruggedized form required to handle greatly expanded throughput or use in diverse settings, nor was the available equipment designed for use by non-specialists or first-responders. Extraordinary effort was needed to alter the situation. NIST was called upon to provide its technical expertise and leadership.

---

[7] U.S. Department of Homeland Security, *National Planning Scenarios*, March, 2005, "Scenario 11: Radiological Attack – Radiological Dispersal Devices," pp. 11-1 – 11-8.

Figure 2R. Cargo screening equipment installed at an airport facility.

Origin of the Effort

To address the looming problem described above, DHS called on experts from NIST, the private sector, and other government organizations to "fast-track" a number of critical radiation detection equipment and equipment training standards through the Institute of Electrical and Electronics Engineers (IEEE), Radiation Detection Standards Program. The primary N42 Committee, chaired by NIST experts, oversaw and coordinated the work of subcommittees N42.RM (Radioactivity Measurements), N42.RPI (Radiation Protection Instrumentation), N42.HSI (Homeland Security Instrumentation), and working groups.

Through the efforts of a diverse group of stakeholders, IEEE's ANSI-accredited National Committee on Radiation Instrumentation developed a suite of consensus standards for personal radiation detectors, portable radiation detection instrumentation, hand-held instruments for detection and identification of radioactive materials, radiation detecting portal monitors, mobile and transportable radiation monitors, training for radiation detection instrumentation, performance criteria for spectroscopy-based portal monitors, performance criteria for active detection systems, and standard data formats for instrument read-outs.

The initial stage in the development of the standards covered the period from 2002-2004. After development and use of testing and evaluation protocols based on these standards, they were revised from 2004-2006. Table 1R lists the suite of radiation detection standard currently available to users and vendors of radiation detection equipment.

Table 1R. IEEE's Radiation Detection Standards

- 42.32 American National Standard Performance Criteria for Alarming Personal Radiation Detectors for Homeland Security
- 42.33 American National Standard for Portable Radiation Detection Instrumentation for Homeland Security
- 42.34 American National Standard Performance Criteria for Hand-Held Instruments for the Detection and Identification of Radionuclides
- 42.35 American National Standard for Evaluation and Performance of Radiation Detection Portal Monitors for Use in Homeland Security 42.37 American National Standard for Training Requirements for Homeland Security Purposes Using Radiation Detection Instrumentation for Interdiction and Prevention
- 42.38 American National Standard Performance Criteria for Spectroscopy-Based Portal Monitors Used for Homeland Security
- 42.41 American National Standard Minimum Performance Criteria for Active Interrogation Systems Used for Homeland Security
- 42.42 American National Standard Data Format Standard for Radiation Detectors Used for Homeland Security
- 42.43 American National Standard Performance Criteria for Mobile and Transportable Radiation Monitors Used for Homeland Security

NIST Gets Involved

Representatives of the Ionizing Radiation Division of NIST's Physics Laboratory have been involved with ANSI and IEEE in the development of numerous consensus standards over the years. N42, the ANSI-IEEE committee for the development of radiation instrumentation standards, was chosen as the lead for this effort because of its ability to rapidly produce the desired standards. As part of its ongoing support for voluntary standards development, NIST personnel chaired the committee at the time of the DHS initiative At the time the fast track effort was initiated, a number of ANSI and ASTM standards were in place for similar applications in the health physics arena, but none of them covered the requirements needed for their use either by non-highly trained individuals nor for the additional environmental and mechanical ruggedness requirements inherent in homeland security applictions.

The standards that emerged in 2004 were subjected to two rounds of DHS-funded testing. The testing results were used by testing labs to evaluate instruments, by manufacturers to improve their product to be able to meet the requirements set by the standards that apply to homeland security applications, and by users for instrument procurement purposes. After the initial development, validation and implementation of these standards, and the failure of any of the equipment to meet them, the manufacturers began developing new equipment and, through an iterative process with industry, the standards were further refined.

This resulted in the establishment of the Graduated Rad/Nuc Detector Evaluation and Reporting (GRaDER) program, which establishes the current American National Standards Institute (ANSI) N42 consensus standards as the initial acceptable performance baseline for radiation detectors and lays the groundwork for more detailed instruction to enter the program. The GRaDER program is managed by DHS's Domestic Nuclear Detection Office (DNDO) together with NIST and NIST's National Voluntary Laboratory Accreditation Program (NVLAP) under which laboratories perform independent and consistent testing of the commercial-off-the-shelf radiation detectors.[8] Results of the GRaDER program testing will be made available to law enforcement and first responder agencies to inform their procurement and grant awards processes.

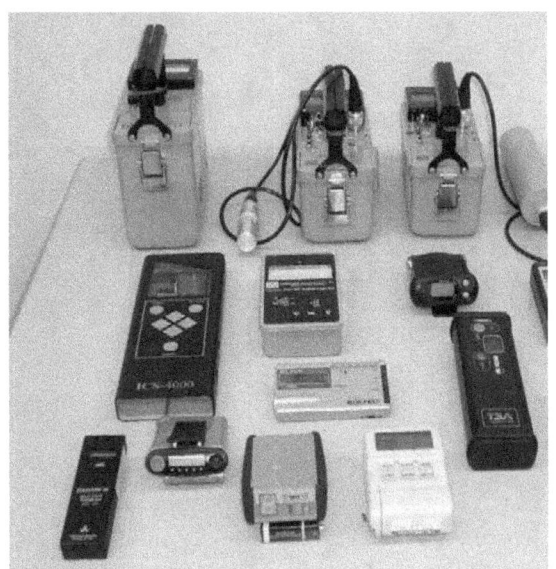

Figure 3R. Handheld radiation detectors.

What would have been done, absent NIST?

Without NIST in the lead, these radiation equipment standards would have taken longer to develop. The fact that NIST is viewed as an impartial participant greatly helped in resolving differences among the various groups involved in the writing of these standards. For all the standards, NIST personnel led the harmonization of the sometimes unrealistic differences between user requirements and the manufacturers' concerns of what present technology can achieve. In addition, NIST provided the means for collaborators to access the information necessary to apply the standards to different types of instruments.

Through its voluntary public-private collaboration, the IEEE's suite of radiation detection standards was developed in under 2 years, at least a year earlier than for a typical documentary standard, and, as a result, problems could be addressed by port personnel in a much more effective manner than they would have been without the standards; industry could develop the new ruggedized and user-friendly detection equipment needed quickly and effectively; and the value added from the sales of new equipment would accrue to industry sooner than it otherwise would have.

From an economic perspective, NIST helped to lower the high transaction costs associated with organizing and harmonizing technical and quality assurance issues among diverse equipment users, designers, and manufacturers.

Conclusion

A joint effort between industry and government agencies to meet the critical DHS objective of increased port security led to the fast-track development of a suite of ANSI accredited documentary standards for radiation detection equipment performance and equipment training. These achievements would not have been achievable in the time accomplished had it not been for NIST's contribution. The economic impacts of these efforts would be measured in terms of shifting a stream of public and private benefits forward in time by

---

[8] The Domestic Nuclear Detection Office (DNDO) was established in 2005 to improve the Nation's capability to detect and report unauthorized attempts to import, possess, store, develop, or transport nuclear or radiological material for use against the Nation, and to further enhance this capability over time.

a minimum of 1 year and in the dramatic reduction in transaction costs that would have been required to harmonize technical differences among the users and designers of new radiation detection equipment. This should result in a system of certified radiation detection equipment that reduces the ability of terrorists to smuggle radioactive material into the United States lowers the risk of the dire consequences depicted in DHS planning scenarios, and increases our sense of security.

X. Materials Declaration Standards to Support Environmental Regulations

Executive Summary

In 2003, the U.S. electronics industry was already struggling with regulations that restricted tin-lead solder and did not focus on looming EU requirements on toxic materials in electronic products, thus finding themselves in a bewildering world of incompatible standards and complicated data exchange tools that threatened to severely impact U.S. high tech exports.

Little progress was being made on creating a Joint Industry Guide (JIG) that could guide industry design and production. Realizing that something needed to be done, in December 2004 NIST organized a meeting with IPC, a global trade association, and iNEMI[9] to discuss the problem and need for a standard way of exchanging JIG and other compliance data. From an initial offer of collaboration, NIST was invited to expand its role and became chair of an international group of government agencies, industry representatives, and technical experts.

NIST guided the group through rigorous and open analyses that recognized and balanced the unique requirements and problems of small, medium, and large manufacturers. The challenges that NIST helped resolve included technical uncertainties, problem modeling, software programming, data standards documentation, and reference implementation. NIST expertise also enabled the group to design innovative ways to use alternative declaration standards, while eliminating many incompatibilities.

The benefits of NIST involvement, like the challenges, were many and varied. NIST was able to reconcile competing approaches in a relatively short time. In only 16 months NIST guided the groups to consensus on the standard and supporting software tools. That short time frame would likely not have been possible without NIST's reputation for impartiality. NIST recognized that the 2004 standard and software would not be the final, but made the solutions easy to maintain and upgrade. From an industry perspective, the relatively speedy resolution and ease of use reduces up-front and compliance costs, a significant factor in the global competitive landscape, especially for smaller companies. Finally, the solution extends to alternative material declaration standards, offering compatibility between complementary standards.

---

[9] International Electronics Manufacturing Initiative

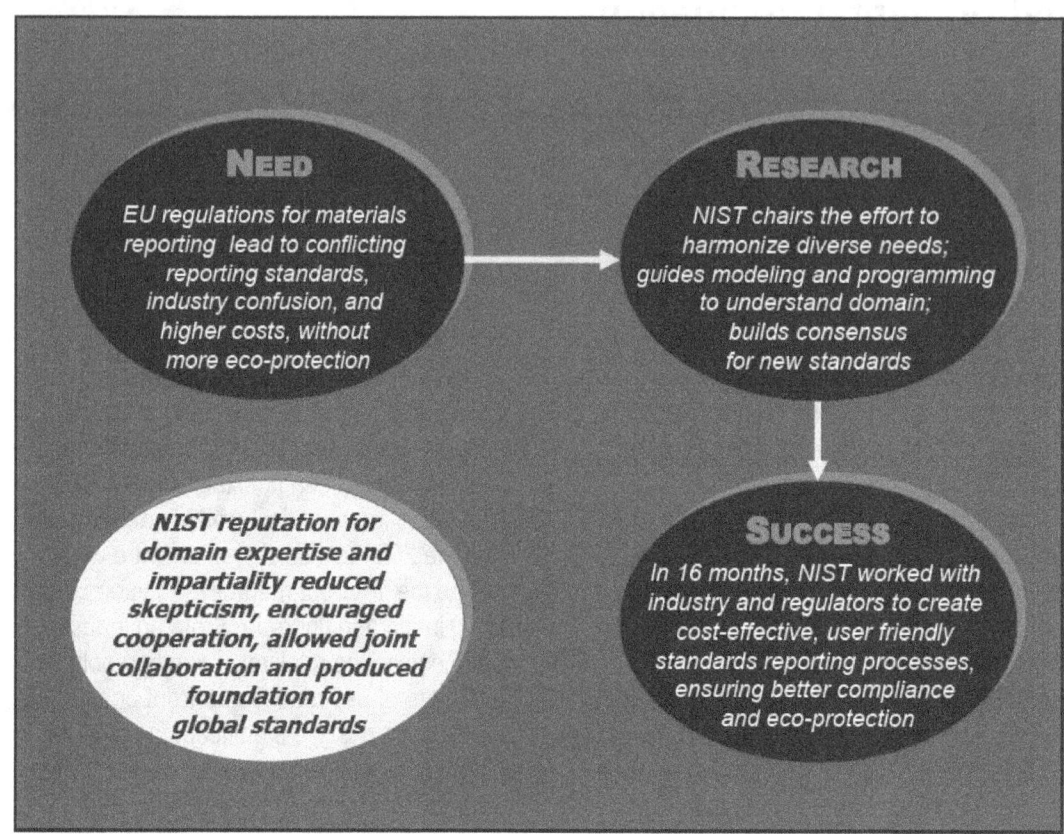

Figure 1M: NIST has positive impact on standards development process

Introduction

The Restriction on Hazardous Materials (RoHS) regulations recently adopted by the European Union (EU) and other U.S trading partners require significantly reduced maximum allowable concentrations of toxic chemicals in electronic products. Companies seeking market entry for consumer electronic and electrical products require stringent materials declarations from their suppliers at all levels of the supply chain.

RoHS regulations affect the worldwide market for "electrotechnical" products, a multi-billion dollar annual market. U.S. companies are significant exporters of these products and must comply with RoHS regulations by replacing components and designing new manufacturing processes to accommodate new or modified raw materials. The European Union (EU) is by far the largest export market for U.S. high-tech electronic goods with $46 billion dollars exported in 2006.[10]

This issue crosses company, industry, domestic, and international lines so that a collective approach to addressing the exchange of compliance data in the new

---

[10] Source: AEA News, "U.S. Technology Exports Up by $21 billion in 2007", July 17, 2007

RoHS regulations was needed. The initial standard that emerged from the undertaking was the IPC 1752, Materials Declaration Management. IPC is a global trade association focused on the electronic interconnection industry.[11]

Origin of the Effort

An increased focus on recycling electronics led the European Union in 2003 to issue the Waste Electrical and Electronic Equipment (WEEE) Directive. The directive set collection, recycling, and recovery targets for all types of electrical goods. This was further expanded to restrict certain hazardous substances and the European Union's new Restriction of Hazardous Substance (RoHS) Directive was implemented on July 1, 2006. To ensure compliance with both Directives the electronics industry needed to be able to track the material composition of the final products being introduced to the EU before the July 1st date. US industry was already struggling with the technical challenges of replacing tin-lead solder in its electronics products and processes. Other than a few large U.S. companies, there was little awareness within the U.S. electronics industry of the new EU emphasis on data exchange needs. For both these reasons, implementation efforts in the United States languished until 2004. Efforts to develop the Joint Industry Guide (JIG) which provides guidance to industry on what materials and substances are to be disclosed by suppliers of electronic and electrical products had begun, and some individual companies and software providers had developed non-standard non-compatible data exchange tools, the proliferation of which actually increased industry's burden of compliance.

Realizing that something needed to be done, in December 2004 NIST organized a meeting with IPC and the International Electronics Manufacturing Initiative (iNEMI) to discuss the problem and need for a standard way of exchanging JIG and other compliance data.[12] As a result, IPC created a new ANSI-approved material declaration standards development project with NIST providing the technical leadership. The 1752 standards development team consisted of IPC staff members, industry representatives from TI, Sun, E2Open, and staff from the Semiconductor Electronics Division of NIST's Electronics and Electrical Engineering Lab.

NIST's Role

NIST and IPC started collaboration in early December 2004, with other participants joining in shortly afterward. IPC created the standards working group and worked to pull in individual companies to provide the domain expertise needed. NIST provided the technical expertise, problem modeling, programming for an associated software application, documentation for an XML data standard, and eventually chaired the effort. The development work included creating the new documentary standard as well as a software reference implementation that could be used by industry. This was especially beneficial for small and medium manufacturers.

In addition to its role supporting the IPC standard effort, NIST also supported the efforts of alternative material declaration standards, most notably RosettaNet and IEC TC111. The IPC 1752 standard was

---

[11] Founded in 1957 Institute for Printed Circuits the industry association changed its name to the Institute for Interconnecting and Packaging Electronic Circuits and, in 1999, to IPC.

[12] iNEMI is an industry-led consortium whose mission is to assure leadership of the global electronics manufacturing supply chain. It has a membership that includes electronics manufacturers, suppliers, associations, government agencies and universities.

designed so that data could be easily imported into a RosettaNet enterprise management system. Also, the model underlying 1752 was used a starting point for the IEC TC111's standard 62474. This allowed the IEC TC111 to leverage the work already done in 1752, greatly diminishing incompatibilities between the two standards going forward.

What would have been done, absent NIST?

NIST's participation accelerated the process both because NIST was a ready source of technical expertise *and* because NIST's "honest broker" role reduced what economists refer to as the "transaction costs" of negotiating complex technical agreements among competing interests. NIST participation improved the technical veracity of the effort, reduced the cost to industry of getting a standard approach in place, and, most importantly, accelerated the flow of economic benefits that result from the implementation of solutions to such problems.

The IPC 1752 working group managed to create the new standard from start to finish in 16 months, releasing both the standard and software tools in April 2006. A second version will soon support a broader scope and can be used for REACH and China ROHS.

From an economic impact perspective, this time saving is critical. Compliance with the EU standard was essential. Even without NIST participation, an approach to material declaration standards for electronic products would have been developed. In fact a number of competing approaches had been developed. The longer the industry went without a common standard, the harder and more costly it would have been to adopt standard practices. *NIST provided technical leadership and an "honest broker" function* that would have been time consuming and costly for industry to replicate.

Second, in addition to accelerating the standard development process *NIST's modeling and software development experts improved the quality of the 1752 standard* by ensuring that it captured the appropriate scope and needs. Industry did not have the XML schema and programming resources needed to develop the solution in the given timeframe and it is unlikely that a broadly compatible technology such as XML would have been selected. The NIST approach was based on rigorous software development processes for data exchange standards that included: defining scope, business cases, and use cases up front, then using modeling to understand the domain, and finally generating the data exchange standard itself from the models. This approach ensured that the final standard more accurately captured the needs of industry, was easy to maintain and update, and could be integrated in data management solutions with minimum effort.

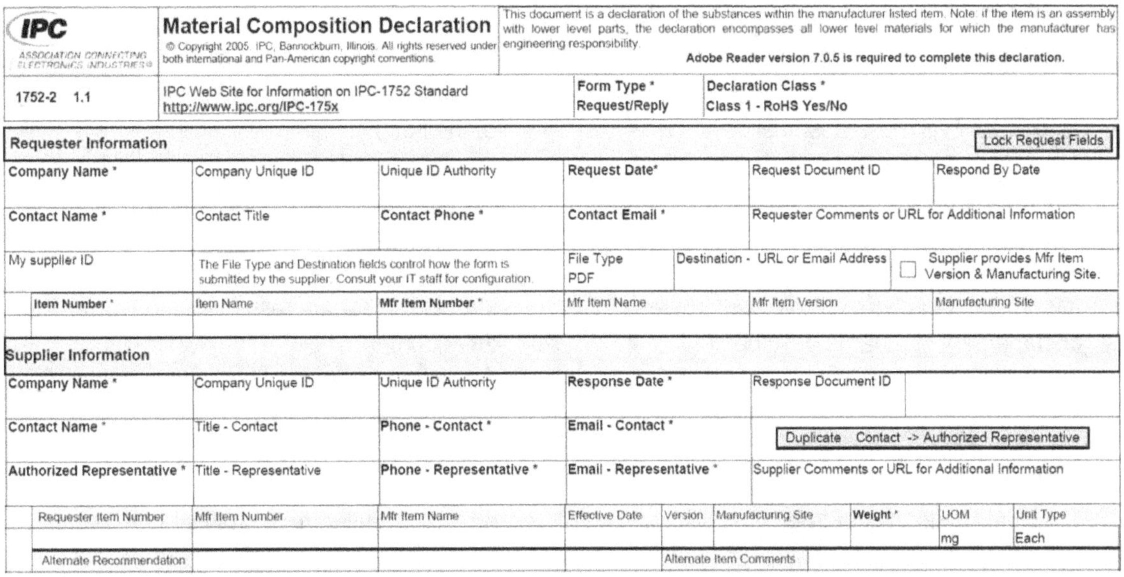
IPC
ASSOCIATION CONNECTING ELECTRONICS INDUSTRIES®
Material Composition Declaration
© Copyright 2005 IPC, Bannockburn, Illinois. All rights reserved under both international and Pan-American copyright conventions.
This document is a declaration of the substances within the manufacturer listed item. Note: if the item is an assembly with lower level parts, the declaration encompasses all lower level materials for which the manufacturer has engineering responsibility.
Adobe Reader version 7.0.5 is required to complete this declaration.
1752-2 1.1
IPC Web Site for Information on IPC-1752 Standard
http://www.ipc.org/IPC-175x
Form Type * Request/Reply
Declaration Class * Class 1 - RoHS Yes/No

Requester Information
Lock Request Fields
Company Name * | Company Unique ID | Unique ID Authority | Request Date* | Request Document ID | Respond By Date
Contact Name * | Contact Title | Contact Phone * | Contact Email * | Requester Comments or URL for Additional Information
My supplier ID | The File Type and Destination fields control how the form is submitted by the supplier. Consult your IT staff for configuration. | File Type PDF | Destination - URL or Email Address | Supplier provides Mfr Item Version & Manufacturing Site.
Item Number * | Item Name | Mfr Item Number * | Mfr Item Name | Mfr Item Version | Manufacturing Site

Supplier Information
Company Name * | Company Unique ID | Unique ID Authority | Response Date * | Response Document ID
Contact Name * | Title - Contact | Phone - Contact * | Email - Contact *
Duplicate Contact -> Authorized Representative
Authorized Representative * | Title - Representative | Phone - Representative * | Email - Representative * | Supplier Comments or URL for Additional Information
Requester Item Number | Mfr Item Number | Mfr Item Name | Effective Date | Version | Manufacturing Site | Weight * | UOM | Unit Type
mg | Each
Alternate Recommendation | Alternate Item Comments

Figure 2M: IPC 1752 tool screen shot showing Class 1& 2 declarations

The net difference between the cost to NIST of participating in the effort and *what it would have cost industry to replicate the functionality and quality of NIST's participation* is an important measure of NIST's economic impact.

Third, *IPC 1752 reduced the cost of compliance* by providing a data exchange standard and freely available software tools. Prior to 1752, compliance was a labor-intensive processes requiring the operation and staffing of phone banks and the compilation of spreadsheets to answer customer requests for information. By accelerating the IPC 1752 development process, the compliance cost savings accrued to industry sooner than they would have otherwise, and could be construed as a benefit uniquely attributable to NIST's participation.

Fourth, the high cost of compliance may have forced some small manufacturers out of the business. To the extent that the *lower cost of compliance allowed small manufacturers to continue operation*, the value added that would have accrued to firms forced to exit the business during the acceleration time attributable to NIST's involvement, so can be construed as an economic impact attributable to NIST.

Fifth, some spillover benefits may have accrued to NIST's involvement in the IPC 1752 development effort to the extent that NIST's methodology served as an example to industry of how to use a rigorous development approach for creating standards that could provide similar results if used for other data exchange standards.

Finally, NIST also participated in alternative material declaration standards, notably the Rosettanet and IEC TC111 efforts. By participating in the initial efforts of these other groups, NIST was able to ensure a high degree of compatibility between the standards. Due to NIST efforts the Rosettanet, IEC TC111, and IPC material declaration standards are all based on the same underlying data model, greatly improving interoperability among the standards. If NIST had not engaged in these activities, the new environmental standards would be largely incompatible; the various efforts would have duplicated efforts to develop underlying data models; and the implementation times would likely have been extended.[13] All these eventualities have associated economic costs. To the extent that they were (or will be) mitigated by NIST's involvement, these reduced costs can also be construed as economic benefits attributable to NIST's involvement in the documentary standards development process.

Conclusion

The dual challenges of trade globalization and the globalization of environmental consciousness pose difficult technical issues for U.S. manufacturers, especially small and medium sized manufacturers. The EU's recently adopted Restriction on Hazardous Materials (RoHS) regulations are emblematic of these trends. U.S. companies are significant participants in the a multi-billion dollar annual market for "electrotechnical" products and now require stringent materials declarations from their suppliers at all levels of the supply chain.

In cooperation with industry NIST has taken a technical leadership role in the development of voluntary documentary standards that address these concerns. The development of IPC 1752, Materials Declaration Management, is exemplary. By providing unique reputational and technical expertise to this effort, NIST's investments have led to economic impacts in the form of process acceleration, quality improvement, reduced costs of compliance, support of small business, and improved interoperability.

---

[13] As of August 2008, the IEC TC111 standard is not yet available.

XI. Future Steps and Conclusion

Technology Services has launched a long-term effort to assess the extent, nature, and outcomes of NIST's involvement in documentary standards development activities. The initial and on-going canvassing activities (as reported in this paper) are part of three-step approach to thoroughly understanding NIST's role in these activities and their impact, with the long-term goal of developing an assessment capability and integrating it into NIST's planning, evaluation, and resource allocation cycle. The benefits from NIST involvement include producing standards faster than otherwise would have been the case without NIST participation; creating specific improvements to products and services; and developing broader standards. We have also learned that the efforts cut across many application areas and technologies.

Some broad findings from this study to date are:

- NIST personnel are a ready source of information needed to screen documentary standards projects for their economic impact potential.

- On the basis of experience conducting outcome assessments, "indicators" can be formulated that aid in the selection of outcome assessment candidates

- On the basis of a straightforward interrogatory process of questions and answers with NIST personnel, "success stories" can be developed that at least illuminate NIST's unique role in the development process and at best clarify both the basis of an activity's economic impact and the sources of evidence that can be used to develop formal, quantitative economic impact assessments.

The three cited success stories also show us concretely how NIST was involved in supporting the development of some important standards, what its role was vis-à-vis industry input in developing the standard, and some concrete outcomes in terms of lives saved and injuries prevented, reduced risk of terrorist actions, and industry-wide transaction cost savings.

From the 78 projects identified in this canvassing effort, one or two will be chosen as case study candidates. A project will be selected based on indications that substantial market impact has occurred or is likely in the near future[20] The perceived importance of NIST's contribution to the standardization effort will also be considered in the selection of the case study.

These studies should yield analytical methodologies that will support NIST efforts to implement a more strategic approach to its standards efforts, including more alignment with government-wide or NIST priority or focus areas. The studies will also enhance NIST's ability to better support industry, government and other stakeholders by participating in standards areas that are most likely to result in safer, more reliable, interoperable products and enhanced U.S. global competitiveness and innovation.

Although a full canvassing report is not necessary each year, the contents of Table 5 could be updated on an annual basis to keep this listing current. Such updating would serve to emphasize that participation in documentary standards activities is an important component of NIST's mission.

In conclusion, the canvassing results presented in Table 5 reflects NIST's important work in supporting standards development activities and how these efforts result in broad-based economic and social benefits. This information also forms the foundation for future work in assessing the extent, nature, and outcomes of NIST's involvement in documentary standards efforts to help promote U.S. innovation and industrial competitiveness.

Table 5. Canvassing Results: NIST Supported Documentary Standards Efforts Having High Impact

Lab	Title	Description	Impact	SDO	Contact	Completed?
BFRL	Fire/Smoke Detectors	NIST has been key player in research and standards work for smoke detector tests. Levels of protection standard and Indiana Dunes Tests are key achievements.	Cut loss of life by 50 % between 1975 and 1998. Adoption of standards and codes internationally.	NFPA UL (1974)	Dick Bukowski	Yes
BFRL	Standard Fire Service Interface	Cooperative program with fire alarm industry for interface to fire departments. NIST is leading the collaboration as well as the effort to write standard	Potential for improved public safety in large commercial buildings. Being implemented by large integrators but standards has not been sold in large numbers yet. City of Boston to mandate its use. Enabling technology for related applications.	NFPA (2002) NEMA (2005)	Dick Bukowski	Yes
BFRL	WTC investigation impacts	As a result of the extensive WTC investigation, 30 specific code change recommendations have been made. 19 proposed changes to model building codes have been submitted to the ICC. Standards will also be revised	Improved building and occupant safety through stronger building codes and standards will result in improved public safety.	ASTM (2006)	Dick Bukowski	No (standards efforts ongoing)

Lab	Title	Description	Impact	SDO	Contact	Completed?
BFRL	Standard Guide for Development of Standard Data Records for Computerization of Thermal Transmission Test Data for Thermal Insulation	In the 1990s, NIST developed Standard Reference Database 81, "*NIST Heat Transmission Properties of Insulating and Building Materials.*" Recognizing that continued development in this area required a standard recording format, NIST was a driving force behind the development of a standardized recording format within ASTM Sub-committee C16.30. This standard, C 1558, is the latest contribution made by NIST to C16. NIST's involvement in C16 has spanned over 60 years. C1558 includes the following standards on the guarded-hot-plate apparatus: Test Method C 177, Practice C 1043; and Practice C1044.	Guide 1558 is the first step in establishing interoperability among the thermal insulation user community in exchanging thermal transmission test data from standard test methods. This standard can be utilized by manufacturers internally to compare process specifications and externally to exchange data with clients or other interested parties.	ASTM	Robert Zarr	Yes
BFRL	Ventilation for Acceptable Indoor Air Quality	NIST was involved in a major revision of the 1989 version of ASHRAE 62.1, which took 12 years to complete. The goal of was to update the technical content of the standard as well as to convert the standard into mandatory and enforceable language suitable for adoption into building codes and other appropriate regulations. NIST contributed its ventilation and indoor air quality expertise to the process and provided leadership to the committee.	This standard is leading to improved indoor air quality buildings, which in turn has been shown to reduce health care costs and improve occupant productivity. The new format of the standard (i.e., the use of normative language) is also helpful to designers and manufacturers because it makes compliance and enforcement much more predictable.	ASHRAE	Andy Persily	Yes

38

Lab	Title	Description	Impact	SDO	Contact	Completed?
BFRL	Methods of Testing and Rating Electrically Driven Unitary Air-Conditioning and Heat Pump Equipment	ASHRAE Standard 37 and 116 describe the test methods – both primary and confirming – used to measure the steady-state cooling and heating capacities of conventional air conditioners and heat pumps and then how that data is used to predict seasonal performance. NIST took a lead role on Standard 37, in particular because of NIST's unique and long-standing role of developing and maintaining the technical content of federally mandated air conditioner and heat pump testing and rating requirements, which reference consensus standards like ASHRAE Stds 37 and 116 to the extent feasible.	The standard – that provides both primary and confirming test methods – acts as the basis for the different performance ratings used to compare and market the millions of air conditioners and heat pumps sold in the United States and Canada each year. With regard to Standard 37, had NIST not participated, the extent of the revisions and updates would have been considerably less and the public review process would have taken several more months.	ASHRAE (2005)	Brian Dougherty	Yes – Standard 37; No – Standard 116
BFRL	Air Conditioning and Heat Pump Testing and Rating Standards	ISO 5151 Non-ducted Air Conditioner and Heat Pumps; ISO Standard 13253, Ducted Air Conditioners and Heat Pumps; ISO Standard 15042, Multi-Split System Air-Cooled Air Conditioners and Air-to-Air Heat Pumps. Each standard covers test methods and rating conditions for both capacity/efficiency tests and pass/fail extreme operations tests. The current drafts of ISO 5151R and 13253R are first revisions of existing standards developed in 1994. NIST took a lead role on the cognizant ISO working group because of interest by both the U.S. Dept. of Energy and U.S. air conditioner and heat pump manufacturers in working towards the adoption of international standards.	These ISO standards are too different from the current U.S. standards to gain immediate adoption. The same condition applies to the European Union that relies on CEN standards. However, the forthcoming ISO standards do provide a target for U.S. standards bodies and CEN to work towards as they periodically revise their own standards. Hopefully, in the future, both the U.S. and the EU will be able to coordinate their respective standards and regulatory bodies to allow adoption of the ISO standards.	ISO	Brian Dougherty	No – All 3 standards are awaiting publication.

Lab	Title	Description	Impact	SDO	Contact	Completed?
BFRL	Fire Test Methods and Standards	Fire research activities have led to the development of ignitibility test methods, surface flammability test methods, furniture flammability test methods, heat release rate test methods, and procedures for measuring the toxicity of combustion products. NIST has lead efforts within the U.S. on fire test standards development.	The number of life loss fires has been significantly reduced over the last several decades. Building materials have better fire resistant properties. Construction practices have changed to reflect a better understanding of unwanted fires, and the ease of ignition. Flammability of furnishings used in offices and homes has been reduced and less toxic building materials and furnishings have been developed. Fire test methods initially developed by NIST are now used nationally and internationally.	ASTM, NFPA, ISO	Randy Lawson	Ongoing
BFRL	Fire Service Standards	NIST has advanced firefighter safety through research on a range of safety issues: personal protective clothing and equipment (PPE); electronic equipment (PASS devices, radios, and thermal imaging systems); automatic water sprinklers; and fire fighter training and suppression tactics. In addition, NIST has produced computer fire simulation capabilities and has used them for the investigation of serious fire incidents. Findings from this research have been coupled with standards for protecting and training fire service personnel.	NIST research on low heat flux burn injuries brought about improvements in NFPA protective clothing standards that affect firefighter safety. This directly influences burn injury rates, monetary losses, and social loss costs to the nation. Work on electronic equipment has brought about changes in standards for PASS devices and radio systems improving their reliability. Research on thermal imaging systems has resulted in a new standard that is also helping to protect firefighters. Computer simulations of firefighter life loss fires have brought about changes in standards for training.	NFPA, ASTM, IFSTA	Randy Lawson Nelson Bryner	Ongoing

Lab	Title	Description	Impact	SDO	Contact	Completed?
BFRL	Slug Calorimeter	NIST has developed a method for testing the thermal conductivity of fire resistive materials used for protecting steel building structures.	Potential for public safety by improving the thermal performance of fire resistive materials.	ASTM (E2584)	Dale Bentz	Yes
BFRL	Laboratory and Field Tests of Adhesion for Fire Resistive Materials	NIST is working on the development of laboratory and field tests of adhesion of fire resistive materials used to protect steel building structures.	Potential to improve public safety by reducing the potential for fire resistive materials to be dislodged from protected steel elements.	ASTM (Committee E6)	Chris White	No
BFRL	16 CFR Part 1633 Standard for the Flammability (Open Flame) of Mattress Sets (Enforced by the Consumer Product Safety Commission)	This standard applies to all residential mattresses sold in this country after July 1, 2007. It seeks to eliminate fire deaths caused by flaming ignition of beds. NIST did all of the technical development work for this safety standard, including a technical assessment of how the number of lives saved was likely to vary with the allowed pass/fail acceptance level of peak heat release rate developed in such fires.	CPSC estimates that the standard has the potential to eliminate about ¾ of the deaths and injuries due to such fires each year in the U.S.	The Sleep Products Safety Council sponsored most of the NIST work. They chose not to submit the test method to ASTM to implement it more rapidly.	Tom Ohlemiller	Yes
BFRL	Sustainable Building	In developing its Building for Environmental and Economic Sustainability (BEES) tool, NIST applied standards for life cycle assessment, life cycle costing, multiattribute decision analysis, and building element classification. Once BEES was published, NIST wrote initial draft of biobased product sustainability assessment standard.	More than 24,000 users of BEES software for building products. BEES also being applied to biobased products as required by federal regulation implementing Section 9002 of the 2002 Farm Bill	ASTM SP D7075 (Evaluating and Reporting Environmental Performance of Biobased Products), ISO	Barbara Lippiatt	Yes

Lab	Title	Description	Impact	SDO	Contact	Completed ?
CSTL	In Vitro Diagnostics (IVD)	U.S. industry came to NIST for help in developing reference measurement procedures and materials for meeting 1998 EU IVD directive. NIST has led the development of the process for review of the "higher order" reference methods and reference materials listed in the JCTLM database of higher order standards and developed and maintains more than half of the approved methods and materials used by industry. NIST is still working with industry in developing documents for traceability and uncertainty within the CLSI and ISO framework.	U.S. industry is world leader in IVD market. NIST leadership within the JCTLM and development of reference methods and materials for clinical diagnostics have assured U.S. industry a level playing field in Europe. U.S firms currently have 60% of the ~$6 billion/year IVD medical device market in Europe.	CLSI ISO (2002)	W.E. May	Yes - but other key related standards still under development
CSTL	Alternative Refrigerants	NIST engaged in research that would allow industry to make the switch to alternative refrigerants in a timely and economic fashion to meet the timetable imposed by the Montreal Protocol of 1987 to develop alternatives to CFCs. NIST researchers developed the REFPROP database which contains precompetitive properties data so that industry could design their own proprietary CFC alternatives. ISO has incorporated this into their standard.	A comparison of industry benefits with the funding stream of NIST's research program estimated a social rate of return of at least 433 % and a BC ratio of 4 to 1 (1998 study).	ISO (2004)	Mark Mclinden	Yes

Lab	Title	Description	Impact	SDO	Contact	Completed?
CSTL	Restriction of certain Hazardous Substances in Electronic Products (RoHS)	NIST is Working with IEC TC111 Working Group 3 drafting and validating IEC CDV 62321, a set of standard test methods for hazardous products for hazardous substances. NIST also holds membership in ASTM International Committee F40, which is developing standard test methods for hazardous substances in raw materials used in the electronics industry.	Standard test methods are needed for companies in the electronic and electrical products manufacturing supply chain to enable them to make accurate declarations of hazardous substances content and shield themselves from the risk of being banned from markets and fined. Supports U.S. competitiveness in the EU, China and other markets.	IEC and ASTM International	Steve Wise	Ongoing. More validation studies required. Expected to be converted to final draft international standard in Dec. 2007
CSTL	Cement and Concrete	NIST consults with ASTM Committee C01 on test methods for cement, concrete, and their ingredients. NIST cement SRMs in the 1880a series support ASTM Standard C 114 for testing of hydraulic cement.	The Cement and Concrete Reference Laboratory (an ASTM research partnership with NIST) uses C 114 and NIST SRMs to qualify all U.S. cement industry labs and many government transportation labs for analyses of cement and concrete.	ASTM International	John Sieber	Ongoing
CSTL	Metals, Ores, and Related Materials	NIST participates in the activities of ASTM Committee E01 under an MOU guiding the development of SRMs for the mining and metals industries.	Standards development and related SRMs improve the quality of metals and alloys used in aerospace, transportation, defense, electronics, human health and safety, and many other applications.	ASTM International	John Sieber	Ongoing

43

Lab	Title	Description	Impact	SDO	Contact	Completed ?
EEEL	Supply chain communication standards	NIST has been instrumental in efforts to develop Product Data Exchange (PDX), RosettaNet interchange specifications (clusters 2 and 7), and Computer-Aided Manufacturing Exchange (CAMX).	Standards support shop floor integration of equipment from different manufacturers and support supply chain communication. These standards are now used in hundreds of thousands of monthly business transactions.	IPC RosettaNet	Barbara Goldstein, John Messina	Yes
EEEL	Broadband (WiMax) Wireless Standards	NIST has been at forefront of developing common open standards for the emerging broadband wireless network technologies. 12 standards projects have been completed with 5 more in development. The standards are widely supported in Asia, and Europeans have elected to follow 802.16. The 802.16e standard (2/06) was major achievement to support mobile terminals	The development of these standards advances the prospects for U.S. technology developers and promotes opportunities for greater access to broadband services. Very broad and fast adoption. Four of the standards were in the top 100 list of IEEE downloads for March 2006. The WiMax Forum with over 350 members was established to promote and certify broadband wireless products.	IEEE (2004) ITU (2006)	Roger Marks	Yes
EEEL	Restriction of Certain Hazardous Substances in Electronic Products (ROHS)	NIST was instrumental in facilitating the development of a Materials Declaration Management standard (consisting of UML model, XML schema and 2 interactive PDF forms) necessary for U.S. companies to show compliance with an EU directive, which bans electrical products exceeding the specified threshold amounts for 6 hazardous substances used in electronics.	Any company that sells an electrical product in EU member nations after 7/1/06 must declare the hazardous content information. NIST work is assisting U.S. industry to stay competitive in Europe, and has promoted information exchange between large and small firms.	IPC (2006) (also iNEMI)	Eric Simmon	Yes, also ongoing

Lab	Title	Description	Impact	SDO	Contact	Completed ?
EEEL	Electromagnetic compatability (EMC)	NIST provides technical leadership in developing standards and improving the measurement methodologies. NIST assists companies to better conduct electro-magnetic measurements by developing alternative EMC test methods.	EMC standards are important for the domestic and export electronics industry. NIST is helping to harmonize U.S. and international standards to reduce the compliance burden on U.S. industry. Informal reports from an aircraft manufacturer suggest that NIST-developed reverberation techniques (implemented in large hangars) alone will at least halve EMC test time for production airliners saving several hundred thousand dollars for each plane tested.	ANSI SAE CISPR IEC	Perry Wilson	Yes, also ongoing
EEEL	Superconductivity Standards	NIST has led IEC's superconductivity standards efforts leading to the first IEC international standard on superconductivity (1998). 13 standards in total have been developed plus one standard on terms and definitions. Inter-laboratory comparisons are ongoing for future standards.	By encouraging international participation in the standards process, NIST has helped U.S manufacturers be competitive in a market dominated by Europe and Japan. MRI is the largest commercial user of superconductivity, and demonstration projects are happening in power grids.	IEC (1998)	Loren Goodrich	Yes, also ongoing
EEEL	Performance standards for metal detectors	NIST/OLES developed new standards for metal detectors used in concealed weapon and contraband detection, along with evaluation and testing criteria and user guides to facilitate implementation.	New standards were used to define requirements for testing of detectors at airports. Standards in use by FAA, TSA and Bureau of Prisons have contributed significantly to the security of U.S.	NIJ (2000) IPC	Nick Paulter	Yes, also ongoing

Lab	Title	Description	Impact	SDO	Contact	Completed ?
EEEL/TS	Performance standards for body armor	NIST/OLES was key driver in developing standard for Ballistic Resistance of Personal Body Armor standard adopted by NIJ. Standard specifies minimum performance requirements and associated test methods. The body armor program is part of NIJ's successful Law Enforcement and Corrections Standards and Testing Program, through which companies may have their products voluntarily certified as compliant with the standard.	Ballistic-resistant body armor meeting NIST-developed performance standards has been credited with saving more than 2500 lives. The Bulletproof Vest Partnership is key stakeholder. Since 1999, over 11 900 jurisdictions have participated in the BVP Program, with $173 million in federal funds committed to support the purchase of an estimated 450 000 vests.	NIJ (2001 most recent) ASTM	Kirk Rice / Gordon Gillerman	Yes, also ongoing
EEEL	Standard Test Methods for MEMS	NIST did pioneering standards work in developing the first standard test methods for MEMS in 2002, with validating round robin studies for these standards completed in 2005. New MEMS/NEMS standards are currently being developed.	MEMS industry has suffered from a lack of standardization. This will allow manufacturers to confirm good performance of products and facilitate international commerce in MEMS.	ASTM (2002, 2005	Janet Marshall	Yes, also ongoing
EEEL	Land-mobile radio interoperability standards	NIST/OLES has been very involved in supporting development of interface standards since 2005 (Project 25). Four of a total of 8 interface standards have been completed. OLES is working to develop a P-25 compliance assessment program.	Allows for better communication amongst law enforcement officials and first responders. Secretary Chertoff made positive comment. Public safety agencies are requiring the new standards in RFPs, but still need 12-18 months to measure impact.	TIA (2005) (3 new standards in past 15 months)	Derek Orr	In progress

Lab	Title	Description	Impact	SDO	Contact	Completed?
EEEL	Flat panel display standards	NIST developed the Flat Panel Display Measurements Standard offered by the Video Electronics Standards Association (VESA). The FPDM is a display-metrology document that serves industry and other standards organization by providing detailed measurement methods, diagnostics, cautions, and tutorial information to assist those concerned about measuring displays.	These standards support commerce and use of flat panel displays by U.S. industry, which is the largest worldwide end consumer of displays.	ISO, VESA, ANSI-Human-Factors-Society Standard, IEEE, and Society of Motion Picture and Television Engineers (SMPTE).	Paul Boynton	Yes, also ongoing
EEEL	Optical fiber telecommunications	NIST provided technical leadership and evaluations for a number of measurement standards related to optical fiber and instrumentation (power meters, optical spectrum analyzers, etc.)	This work resulted in numerous documentary standards, round robin evaluations, and SRMs that accelerated the adoption of optical fiber communications.	TIA FO-4 IEC TC86	Tim Drapela	Yes, and ongoing
EEEL	High-Frequency Dielectric Measurement Standard	NIST performed the necessary metrology and theory to develop the split-post method to the point of industry acceptance and a standard measurement method	As frequencies of operations of microelectronics increases, the need for well-characterized measurement methods from 7 to 60 Ghz increases. This method satisfies the need.	IPC 2006 (ANSI, IEC in near-future)	James Baker-Jarvis	Yes
ITL	Digital Encryption Standard (DES) and Advanced Encryption Standard (AES)	NIST developed DES standard to support electronic transactions and implemented conformance testing. In 1997, NIST announced initiation of the effort to replace DES with a new advanced encryption module, which implements symmetric key cryptography. Implemented as FIPS standards in 2001.	DES was critical in launching the commercial encryption industry. Users realized significant operational efficiencies, and DES was critical to rise of electronic banking. Since introduction of AES, approximately 200 AES products have been approved.	FIPS 46 (1977) 46-3 (1999) 197 (2001)	Mike Hogan	Yes

Lab	Title	Description	Impact	SDO	Contact	Completed ?
ITL	Role Based Access Control (RBAC)	Lack of standardization was hampering growth of access control products. NIST supplied infrastructure tools to support industry and provided demonstrations of implementations.	NIST's involvement accelerated RBAC by 1 year and lowered R&D costs for software vendors by 6 percent. RTI estimates $671M Net Present Value to economy. Previously studied by Program Office.	INCITS 359 (2003)	Mike Hogan	Yes
ITL	Biometrics	This is an umbrella category covering a number of standards initiatives. NIST/ITL is a major contributor to the national and international biometrics programs by providing leadership for the two standards bodies (INCITS M1 and JTC 1 SC 37), by chairing development of biometric application profiles through these SDOs, and by providing technical editors and a number of technical experts to both SDOs. INCITS, as well as JTC 1 SC 37, are approaching completion of the first generation of biometric data interchange formats for a number of biometric modalities and other biometric standards. Fifteen American National Standards and ten International standards have been published to date.	Many of the first generation of data interchange format standards have already been adopted by large users of personal authentication applications ranging from financial transactions to visitor authentication in amusement parks. Examples of adoption include DHS's adoption of the face recognition standard (INCITS 385) and INCITS 383 (Information technology - Application Profile - Interoperability and Data Interchange - Biometric Based Verification and Identification of Transportation Workers) for the TWIC program. Please see end-notes[xxi]	INCITS ISO/IEC	Fernando Podio	Many projects completed, but much work still ongoing
ITL	BioAPI Conformance Test Suite (CTS)	NIST's biometric standards program provides leadership to national and international biometric standards bodies. A key achievement is the development of the BioAPI CTS implementation also known as the Biometric Test Environment.	The BioAPI CTS provides a test methodology for biometric product developers. The biometric industry is growing rapidly in response to homeland security and commercial needs. Over 30 vendors claim products conforming with BioAPI.	INCITS 358	Fernando Podio	Yes

Lab	Title	Description	Impact	SDO	Contact	Completed?
ITL other labs contribute	Health informatics	This is an umbrella category covering a number of standards initiatives. NIST works with industry, government and trade groups to develop metrics to demonstrate software interoperability and conformance to particular standards. Specific activities include: standards harmonization; performance and conformance metrics for HIT; guidelines for telemedicine; and security related activities. NIST has interagency agreement with the ONC.	All anticipated benefits: - consumers can move seamlessly between practitioners; - clinicians have information needed at point of care; - payers benefit from economic efficiencies; - public health benefits; and - less medical errors. (Note: Can expand on individual activities but still early for measuring impact.)	HITSP/ANSI IEEE HL7	Lisa Carnahan	No
ITL	XDS (cross-enterprise document sharing)	This is a component of NIST's overall health informatics effort. NIST was instrumental in developing the ebXML registry standard and now supports IHE in developing their XDS profile that integrates ebXML standard into the health care environment. Also developed a test environment used in IHE Connectathons. Ver 2.1 of standard became ISO 15000.	XDS will be a component of the technical infrastructure for electronic health records. Four large commercial vendors have demo versions and some CCHIT contractors are planning to include in their deliverables. 500 downloads of open source implementation. Expect products and installed based by 2007.	OASIS (2000) ISO IHE, HITSP/ANSI	Bill Majurski	Yes (but extensions still being developed)
ITL	XML Technologies	This is an umbrella category covering a number of Web-based standards, including: XML, XSLT, XSL-FO, DOM, XML Schema and XML Query. NIST is a major contributor to the development of conformance tests for these standards.	NIST tests ensure that XML implementations are accurate and interoperable, providing the foundation for the expansion and widespread use of XML in electronic commerce and enterprise systems. NIST tests have resulted in bug fixes to implementations and corrections to the XML specifications.	W3C	Carmelo Montanez	Yes (but tests for new standards are being developed)

Lab	Title	Description	Impact	SDO	Contact	Completed?
ITL	Voting Systems	In response to the 2002 Help America Vote Act (HAVA), NIST is providing technical expertise and developing voting system guidelines and standards including a uniform set of open tests to replace existing proprietary tests for federal certification. HAVA requires NIST to evaluate testing labs and make recommendations for accreditation.	This will reduce security vulnerabilities and voting system errors and increase voter confidence while maintaining reasonable costs and increasing usability and accessibility to all voters. The first set of testing labs certified in January 2007.	ANSI IEEE Access Board	Mark Skall, John Wack	No
ITL	Personal Identity Verification (PIV)	In response to Homeland Security Presidential Directive-12, NIST developed FIPS 201 and supporting special publications, which specify architecture and requirements for a common ID standard for federal employees and other eligible personnel. The PIV card supports multi-factor authentication and is to be used for control of both physical access to federal facilities and control of logical access to many federal information systems.	Agencies must begin to implement in Oct 2006. Federal smart card market is estimated at approx $6B. Smart card industry is lining up to develop products. Standard will improve security of physical and logical assets and reliability of federal ID credentials. Beginning to replace Eauthentication for internal agency applications. Full implementation required by end-2008.	FIPS 201 (2005)	Bill MacGregor	Yes
ITL	ISO/IEC 24727: Identification cards – Integrated circuit card programming interfaces	Development of a multi-part international standard based on NISTIR 6887. Provides interfaces and application programming interfaces for interoperable use of integrated circuit cards. Dedicated ISO/IEC task force for this work chaired by NIST.	Removal of U.S. barriers to smart card adoption. Solves known technical barriers to interoperable use of integrated circuit cards, in particular as related to identity credentials, such as the Federal PIV card. Receiving world-wide attention, as evidenced by early adoption by the EU and Australia. Improves reliability and portability of security identity credentials; opens markets for U.S. API providers.	ISO/IEC JTC 1 SubCommittee 17	Teresa Schwarzhoff	Part 1: IS 2006 Part 2: IS 2007 Part 3: IS 2008 Part 4: IS 2008 Part 5: IS 2008, 2009

Lab	Title	Description	Impact	SDO	Contact	Completed?
ITL	National technical report: ISO/IEC 24727	Describes the interworking of two integrated circuit card applications on the same card using the ISO/IEC 24727 series of standards. The two card applications used are the U.S. Government's Personal Identity Verification (PIV) card application as described in NIST SP 800-73 and the Fare Payment Card application as described in the INCITS Interoperability Framework for Contactless Fare Payment Technologies and Systems documents. National Task Group responsible for this body of work Chaired by NIST.	Improves U.S. contributions to ISO/IEC 24727 standards to ensure compatibility with U.S. federal standards. Improves commercialization of ICC and related support products. Improves quality of service delivery with identity credentials tokens.	ANSI/INCITS B10	Teresa Schwarzhoff	Fall 2007
ITL	Security Requirements for Cryptographic Modules	NIST developed standard. Cryptographic Module Validation Program created in conjunction with Canadian authorities. FIPS 140-2 has become defacto international standard. Want convergence with FIPS 140-3 and ISO 19790.	FIPS 140-2 is recognized by governments worldwide. Very successful validation program.13 CMVP labs have been accredited by NVLAP. Over 900 certificates have been provided to over 200 different vendors.	FIPS 140-2 (2001) ISO/IEC 19790 (2006 – but some U.S. specific items removed)	Randall J. Easter	Yes
ITL	Grid Computing	To ensure the success of grid computing, grid systems that implement standards solutions will require methods to measure, analyze, and manage increasingly greater numbers of grid resources in order to ensure system reliability under volatile and uncertain conditions.	Metrics for evaluating grid welfare/health will provide the necessary measurement capabilities needed to help accelerate the commercialization and use of commercial grid systems, allow grid users and providers to evaluate operation of grid systems and grid compute economies and improve the OGF standards by providing a measurement basis for evaluation of standards-based grid system components	Open Grid Forum (OGF)	Chris Dabrowski	No

Lab	Title	Description	Impact	SDO	Contact	Completed ?
ITL	MPEG-7	The MPEG-7 standard also known as "Multimedia Content Description Interface" aims at providing standardized core technologies allowing description of audiovisual data content in multimedia environments. This technology is being designed by a range of experts including content creators, broadcasters, manufacturers, publishers, IP rights managers, telecommunication service providers, academia, gov't, etc. NIST is a major contributor for the MPEG-7 Interoperability Testbed provides validation tools for MPEG-7 technology; and is the main editor for creation of MPEG-7 profiles and levels for various application domains. MPEG-7 metadata descriptions are the basic building block to describe audiovisual content so that search engines can index, search, and retrieve more effective and efficient way	NIST M7ITB validator ensures that MPEG-7 description instances are accurate according to the standard specification and interoperable across various vendor implementations. It provides the validation on MPEG-7 schemas and conformance testing on MPEG-7 instances. This technology is applicable for wide spectrum of applications such as: • Broadcast media (e.g., radio and TV); • Digital libraries (e.g., film, image, video and radio archives); • E-Commerce (e.g., advertising, directories of e-shops); • Education (e.g., multimedia courses, on-line training); • Home Entertainment (e.g. home video, game, karaoke); and • Multimedia directory services (e.g. yellow pages, tourist info).	ISO/IEC SC29 WG11	Wo Chang	Yes
ITL	Software engineering: Software product Quality Requirements and Evaluation (SquaRe) – Common Industry Format (CIF) for Usability Test Reports	CIF provides a standard method for reporting usability test findings. The format is designed for reporting results of formal usability tests in which quantitative measurements were collected and is particularly appropriate for summative/comparative testing. The CIF provides guidance on how to report the results of a usability test, not how to conduct them. The CIF targets usability professionals and stakeholders	Stakeholders can use the usability data to help make informed decisions concerning the release or procurement of software products. Vendors and procurers of software systems now have quantitative data on which to base decisions regarding the usability of a product. Raised the visibility of usability of software systems for procurement.	ISO 25062:2005	Mary Theofanos	Yes

Lab	Title	Description	Impact	SDO	Contact	Completed ?
MEL	Standard for the Exchange of Product Model Data (STEP)	Previously well-documented study. STEP suite of standards enables manufacturing companies to exchange digital representations of engineering and manufacturing data. MEL believes revisions, extensions to the standard, and work on testing methodologies still make this relevant. First 12 parts of STEP approved as international standards in 1995. 30 parts approved by 2002, and many more since then.	NPV over $1 billion calculated in previous study. Allows for long-term data archiving. Being used in most key complex manufacturing industries such as automotive, aerospace and ship building. For example, Lockheed plans to use STEP across all new aircraft programs with first tier suppliers and has documented their savings on the F-16 program.	ISO (1995)	Steve Ray	Yes
MEL	Inventory visibility and interoperability	NIST was requested by AIAG to develop a common interface specs and test some OAG standards. Tested multi-tier supply chain standards in auto industry where lack of interoperability costs $1 billion annually. Focused on dimensional metrology systems.	AIAG study shows that implementing NIST/AIAG recommendations from testing study will result in cost avoidance of $197 million and net savings of $255 million.	OAG	Steve Ray	Yes (almost)
MEL	Integrated Sensor Network (RFID)	MEL is working on developing standards for integrated sensor networks containing RFID. Standard still under development.	Industry is looking to incorporate wireless communications into their products and processes. No impact to measure at this time.	IEEE	Kang Lee	No

Lab	Title	Description	Impact	SDO	Contact	Completed?
MEL	Systems Modeling Language (SysML)	The Systems Engineering Modeling Language (SysML) was adopted by the Object Management Group, with major contributions from NIST's Manufacturing Engineering Laboratory. MEL's contributions were in the critical area of process modeling, and in cooperation and liaison with the International Council on Systems Engineering. SysML is a graphical modeling language for specifying, analyzing, designing, and verifying complex manufactured systems that may include hardware, software, information, personnel, procedures, and facilities.	SysML is the first standard systems engineering modeling language, used in the development of large-scale products in the military and industry. It is implemented by several systems modeling companies.	OMG		
MEL	Ontology Definition Metamodel	NIST's Manufacturing Engineering Laboratory managed the entire standard's development cycle -- from conception to adoption by the OMG -- over the last four years. In addition to this leadership, NIST was also a principal technical contributor to the effort, which involved four software providers and other experts throughout the world. The result of this multi-year effort was the international standardization of the Ontology Definition Metamodel, or ODM. The standard supports four existing international standard knowledge representation languages, bringing them together in a common modeling framework.	Reasoning tools can be used to reconcile the terms found in various forms of electronic business transactions, enabling manufacturers to communicate reliably with new software suppliers. With ODM, such communication will not require developing partner-specific translation software, which introduces longer lead times and human errors, and inhibits innovative partnerships. Other than the manufacturing community -- notably the intelligence community, the emergency response community, and the healthcare community -- have similar problems and are	OMG		

Lab	Title	Description	Impact	SDO	Contact	Completed ?
		enabling capabilities for Model Driven Architecture-based software engineering, namely the formal grounding for representation, management, interoperability, and application of business semantics	actively involved in the development, use and exchange of ontologies.			
MEL	Unified Modeling Language	NIST led the introduction of process modeling in the Unified Modelling Language (UML), the globally dominant and information modeling standard in use today. UML models application structure, behavior, and architecture, as well as manufacturing process and structure.	A new generation of software tools, books, and training curricula are based on the process modeling capability introduced in UML 2 under NIST's leadership.	OMG	Conrad Bock	
MEL	Business Process Definition Metamodel (BPDM)	BPDM was adopted by the Object Management Group (OMG), with supporting votes from major business process tool vendors, service providers, and users. Execution-interoperable process models execute the same way for all parties interchanging the model. NIST introduced execution interoperability for the first time in an adopted process model, using advanced metamodeling techniques to ensure compatibility with ISO 18629, Process Specification Language.	BPDM is the first standardized process model designed from the ground up with precise and reliable execution in mind.. NIST received testimonials from major corporations in appreciation of its leadership and technical achievements in this area (e.g., Boeing, Borland, Unisys, Electronic Data Systems, Lombardi, and General Services Administration).	OMG	Conrad Bock	

Lab	Title	Description	Impact	SDO	Contact	Completed?
MEL	Process Specification Language	ISO's Process Specification Language has had its first application to conventional manufacturing process languages, improving the efficiency and reliability of system construction. The PSL standard is a fully axiomatized, first-order logic ontology to support the unambiguous description and exchange of process information. NIST provided the initial draft specifications and technical leadership in having the first 8 parts of ISO 18629 published as International Standards.	It resulted in the first standardized process model designed from the ground up with PSL's precision in mind, in collaboration with the Object Management Group. NIST received testimonials from major corporations in appreciation of its leadership and technical achievements in this area (e.g., Boeing, Borland, Unisys, Electronic Data Systems, Lombardi, and General Services Administration).	ISO	Conrad Bock	
MEL	Quality Measurement Data (QMD)	The QMD spec is the work of the MEPT Quality Measurement (MEQM) working group of the Automotive Industry Action Group (AIAG) Metrology Project Team (MEPT). The goal of the MEQM has been to produce a non-proprietary, computer-readable, and widely implemented standard for the interface between measurement devices (not merely dimensional) and Statistical Process Control (SPC) analysis software packages.	The QMD standard holds promise to save statistical process control (SPC) software industry in the U.S. alone around $50 million over the next few years. This estimate is based on verifiable data from reliable sources.	AIAG	John Horst	Yes, but ongoing efforts on multiple standards are continuing

Lab	Title	Description	Impact	SDO	Contact	Completed?
MEL	Dimensional Interface Measurement Standard (DMIS)	The DMIS standard provides interoperability standards for coordinate measurement machines. NIST has contributed significantly to the standard and produced a suite of conformance testing tools.	The DMIS standard is currently written and read by nearly every Coordinate Measuring Machine (CMM) software vendor worldwide. However, proprietary languages and a variety of incompatible non-complaint DMIS implementations still abound. NIST is providing the first set of tools with which vendors and users can evaluate the conformance of a particular implementation to the DMIS specification.	ISO 22093 Dimension Metrology Standards Consortium	John Horst	Yes, but update efforts are continuing
MEL	Inspection Plus-Plus (I++) Dimensional Measurement Equipment (DME) Standard	The I++ standard provides interoperability standards for coordinate measurement machines. NIST has contributed significantly to the standard and produced a suite of conformance testing tools.	The I++ DME standard is currently written and read by nearly every Coordinate Measuring Machine (CMM) hardware and software vendor worldwide. Incompatible, non-compliant I++ DME implementations are rare due to the influence of NIST early on in the standards development process.	International Association of Coordinate-Measuring-Machine-Manufacturers [NOTE – industry group, not official SDO, although this is treated as a standard]	John Horst	Yes, but ongoing work in progress
MEL	Safety Standard for Guided Industrial Vehicles and Automated Functions of Manned Industrial Vehicles	The safety standard for users and vendors of manned and automated guided vehicles. NIST has contributed significantly to the standard providing performance testing and suggesting improvements to the standard for non-contact safety systems.	The B56.5 standard is currently written and read by forklift and AGV manufacturers and users, mainly in the US. The language was incorporated into the ISO safety standard as well and is being proposed for a global standard.	Material Handling Industry of America (MHIA)	Roger Bostelman	Yes, but ongoing work in progress.

57

Lab	Title	Description	Impact	SDO	Contact	Completed ?
MEL	Industrial Automation & Control Systems Security Standards	MEL is heavily involved in the development of standards for the security of Industrial Automation & Control Systems (IACS). This standards effort encompasses multiple standards inside the ISA-SP99 committee. Securing IACS facilities involves both the development of standards for the technology used to build the IACS and the policies & procedures applied to the IACS. MEL has multiple leadership & editorial roles in the standards committee	Secure the nation's critical infrastructure and manufacturing facilities.	ISA	James Gilsinn	Yes, but ongoing efforts in multiple standards continue
MEL	Industrial Robots and Robot Systems-Safety Requirements	This standard describes the requirements the manufacture, installation, safeguard maintenance and repair of manipulating industrial robots, in order to enhance the safety of personnel using these devises is a very complicated standard that took approximately 10 years to prepare and reach consensus.	This standard has been accepted by users of industrial robots in the US all the manufacturers who sell these devices in the USA. Several years Canada decided to adopt the same standard with some minor changes	Robotic Industries Association/ANSI R15.06-1999	Nicholas G. Dagalakis	Yes
MEL	Robots for Industrial Environment-Safety Requirements Part 1-Robot	ISO has decided to adopt the US ANSI/RIA R15.06-1999 robot safety standard with some modifications, which are dictated by EU relevant laws. The main modification required was to split the standard in two segments, with the first (Part 1) addressing the requirements for the manufacture of manipulating industrial robots and the second for the installation, safeguarding, maintenance and repair of manipulating industrial robots.	No data available since this standard passed balloting only a few month	Robotic Industries Association ANSI RIA/ISO10218-12007	Nicholas G. Dagalakis	To be completed shortly

Lab	Title	Description	Impact	SDO	Contact	Completed?
MEL	Cleaning Method Contamination Assessment for Optical Assembly	The scope of this standard is to describe inspection and cleaning methods for all devices interconnections in order to avoid loss of optical signals.	This standard provides very significant information for the manufacturing functioning and reliable optoelectric devices. The good performance of communication systems, micro devices, sensors, etc., depends on the information provided by this standard.	IPC	Nicholas G. Dagalakis	Yes
MSEL	Charpy Program	Test of brittleness/ductility and impact energy for metals. NIST had instrumental role. Working to harmonize with ISO.	Written into numerous specs. around the world. Key quality test in used in metal contracts. Largest selling Standard Reference Material in MSEL.	ASTM (1970s - 2007) ISO	Chris McCowan/ Tom Siewert	No (ISO harmonization effort still ongoing)
MSEL	Ceramic Mechanical Properties and Specifications	MSEL had lead role in developing 4 generic ASTM and ISO property standards that were later used to make materials specifications for hip-joint ceramic balls and ceramic ball bearings.	Generic standards were included in three hip joint and one ball bearing specification standards. Hip-joint standards have significant health care impact, and ball bearings have large impact on manufacturing.	ASTM (1990-1999) ISO (2000-2001)	George Quinn	~~No~~ Yes
MSEL	Ceramic Armor	NIST developed test method standards and SRMs used by U.S. Army to characterize materials.	Saves warfighter lives.	ASTM (1990-1999)	George Quinn	Yes
MSEL	Hardness Standardization for Metals	NIST was instrumental in the research to establish a traceability system for hardness measurements, developing SRMs and is refining test methods. NIST has most accurate hardness machine in U.S.	Huge impact on trade of metals. Establishes national chain of traceability to fundamental SI units. Disputes between producers and users curtailed. Information gained from NIST's participation in the CIPM has influenced ASTM requirements.	ASTM, ISO (1991-2007)	Sam Low	No, as industrial needs arise, NIST research and interaction with the CIPM and other NMIs continue to influence the SDO standards.

Lab	Title	Description	Impact	SDO	Contact	Completed?
MSEL	Knoop Test for Ceramics	Hardness test invented at NIST (Knoop method) adapted for advanced ceramics.	To be written into USA tariff schedule and under negotiation within NAFTA for items such as ceramic wares for technical uses, kitchen and bath products, and porcelain and china.	ASTM, ISO (1996-2000)	George Quinn	Yes
MSEL	Instrumented Indentation Testing	Standard practice and test methods for instrumented indentation provide first reliable basis for quantitative mechanical property determination for thin films and coatings.	Provides the first basis for product specifications related to coating and thin film hardness and elasticity. Relevant to microelectronics and MEMS components, wear coatings for cutting tools, scratch-resistant optical (eyeglass) coatings, automotive paints, etc.	ASTM, ISO (2002 – 2007)	Douglas Smith	ISO: Parts 1-3 completed, Continuing on for new parts. ASTM – Part 1 completed in 2007. Continuing work on new parts.
MSEL	Test Method for Molecular Mass Distribution of Polystyrene	New ASTM Test Method D 7134 uses matrix assisted laser desorption/ionization mass spectroscopy to determine the molecular mass of polystyrenes	This method will significantly improve the ability of different laboratories to measure compositions of synthetic polystyrenes, which are used for a wide variety of products. There was broad international and industrial support via a 23 lab VAMAS round robin. An ISO standard is in preparation.	ASTM (2005-2007)	Charles Guttman and William Wallace	Completed in ASTM, Ongoing in ISO

Lab	Title	Description	Impact	SDO	Contact	Completed ?
MSEL	Test Methods for Embedded Passive Materials	Master IPC standard TM-650, Test Methods Manual has been expanded with new tests to Determine Permittivity and Loss Tangent of Embedded Passive Materials at High Frequencies. Recently two new standards have been adopted: IPC 4821 is a specification for capacitor materials and contains material designation, conformance (requirements), qualification (characterization) and quality assurance specifications for fabrication of embedded passive capacitor devices. IPC 2316 is a Design Guide that gives manufacturers the necessary information for incorporating embedded passive components into their applications. In addition, it also assists the users in understanding some of the physical and thermal characteristics of the embedded component materials.	New test procedures and specifications are having a major impact on Embedded Passive Electronic materials for wireless communications components and military devices where miniaturization is critical. Improved reliability.	IPC (2005-2007)	Jan Obrzut	Yes, and ongoing
PL	Standard Practice for Obtaining Colorimetric Data from a Visual Display Unit Using Tristimulus Colorimeters ASTM E1255-03	This standard adopted the method developed by NIST researchers and drafted by a NIST researcher. It prescribes the method for measuring chromaticity of displays accurately using tristimulus colorimeters, with computational corrections for errors introduced by imperfect matching of spectral responsivity of the detectors. This method can be applied to measurement of any RGB based color displays.	This standard is helping improve the measurement accuracy for color displays and thus contributing to efficient production, commerce, and quality of display products. Tristimulus colorimeters are widely used in the display industry, but the accuracy has been a problem. This method corrects the errors. Used in some commercial products.	ASTM (2003)	Yoshi Ohno	Yes

Lab	Title	Description	Impact	SDO	Contact	Completed?
PL	Approved Method for Total Luminous Flux Measurement of Lamps Using an Integrating Sphere Photometer	This standard (IESNA LM-78-2006) was drafted by a NIST researcher, and NIST played the leading role in developing this standard. This standard provides recommendations on how to use integrating sphere photometers for accurate measurement of total luminous flux (lumen) of light sources, including design of integrating spheres, recommended sphere geometry, measurement procedures, correction methods, and uncertainty analysis. This document is to be referenced in many other IESNA LM standards.	This standard will help improve the measurement accuracy of total luminous flux (lumen) in lighting industry, thus contributing to efficient production, commerce, and quality of lamp products. This standard is to be referenced by accreditation program for Energy-Efficient Lighting products, and all lamp manufacturers will follow the practice given in this standard.	IESNA (2007)	Yoshi Ohno	Yes
PL	Specifications for the Chromaticity of Solid State Lighting Products	NIST led the development of this standard (ANSI C38.377), which is under final approval. This standard specifies the white light chromaticity ranges for solid state lighting (SSL) products. This standard will ensure that new lighting products using LEDs will have high-quality white light and appropriately classified according to color temperature to allow smooth replacement of traditional light sources or other SSL products having similar color.	DOE is starting the Energy Star program for SSL products, which needs this standard. All SSL products should be designed to meet this standard, and in turn, white LEDs (used for the SSL products) will also be designed and classified for color according to this standard. Thus, this standard will have significant impact on both white LED and SSL industries.	ANSI (2008)	Yoshi Ohno	Yes

Lab	Title	Description	Impact	SDO	Contact	Completed ?
PL	Approved Method for the Electrical and Photometric Measurements of Solid-State Lighting Product	NIST is leading the development of this standard (IESNA LM-79), which is in the final stage. This standard provides standard test methods for measurement of total luminous flux (lumen), electrical parameters, luminous efficacy (lm/W) and color quantities of solid state lighting (SSL) products.	DOE is starting its Energy Star program for SSL products, which needs this standard. An associated laboratory-accreditation program for SSL products is being developed, which refers to these test methods. The SSL manufacturers and testing laboratories will be required to use the test methods specified in this document, and commercial photometric instruments will be designed to comply with this standard.	IESNA	Yoshi Ohno	In final stage
PL	Color Rendition by White Light Sources	NIST is leading the development of this international standard. This standard will replace the CIE Color Rendering Index, which has been used widely over 30 years by lighting industry. A new metric is needed to address the problems of the index with solid-state light sources. Color rendering is a very important property of light sources for lighting, and is also closely related to energy efficiency.	Energy regulations such as the U.S. Energy Policy Act and Energy Star (for fluorescent lamps, and solid state lighting products) require minimum Color Rendering Index as well as minimum lumens per watt for light source products. DOE is waiting to use the new standard for Energy Star. The new standard being developed is expected to improve color quality and energy efficiency of all light sources including SSL products.	CIE	Wendy Davis	No, still in early stage

Lab	Title	Description	Impact	SDO	Contact	Completed ?
PL	Photometry of Flashing Lights	NIST is leading the development of this international standard. This standard will specify the photometric scale for the effective intensity of flashing light used in signaling and warning lights according to temporal human visual sensitivity. This standard will unify different scales used in different countries.	Flashing warning lights are widely used for signaling and warning lights in transportation for aircraft, airport, highways, roads, and buildings. The intensity scale for these flashing lights has never been internationally standardized. The specification of all these flashing lights products will use the effective intensity scale (candela) defined by this standard.	CIE	Yoshi Ohno	In progress
PL	Radiation Detector Certification (Rad-Nuc)	NIST was driving force behind the revision of 4 standards (N42.32-35) related to radiation detector certification for four classes of detectors from hand-held instruments to monitors used for trucks to cargo containers. The team also revised test and evaluation protocols to be used for testing these instruments.	These standards and the associated testing will help improve public safety by addressing performance of detection equipment used in border control, customs, coast guard and postal services and their need for detection of illicit radioactive materials and response to terrorist threats. This work is recognized by DHS as a model for gov't/private sector development of standards for homeland security.	IEEE /ANSI (2005-present)	Mike Unterweger	6 standards have been published, 3 are awaiting publication, and, at least 4 more are under development
PL	Radiation Detector international performance standards	NIST is heavily involved in the development of international standards for radiation detectors for both metrology and security uses.	These standards will lead to improvements in the detection of illicit radioactive materials on the international level.	IEC (2005 – present)	Mike Unterweger	3 standards have been published and several more are in the draft stage.

Lab	Title	Description	Impact	SDO	Contact	Completed ?
PL/TS	X-Ray Security Screening Systems	NIST is leading a program to develop 4 technical performance standards (ANSI N42.44-47) related to the image quality of x-ray security screening systems for cargo, computerized tomography (for checked baggage), checkpoint and body scan. These standards will include test methods, test artifacts, and minimum performance requirements where this does not compromise security sensitive information.	These standards will be used by DHS and state and local governments to insure that only systems that meet satisfactory levels of performance will be purchased and used in the nation's aviation security venues, public buildings and events, and screening at ports, borders, and prisons.	IEEE /ANSI N42.46 (2008) N42.44 (2008)	Larry Hudson	No, remaining in 2009

65

ENDNOTES

[1] It is possible that in some instances a narrower scope might actually serve the market better, but only 4 percent of the respondents indicated that NIST's involvement narrowed the scope of the standard.

[2] Link and Scott distinguish three different approaches to evaluating economic impact: the counterfactual approach, the Grilliches/Mansfield approach, and the spillover approach. The counterfactual approach appears more conservative, in the sense that it accounts for first-order net benefits that accrue to NIST's unique contributions. The availability of new products and services suggests second-order benefits and the application of the Grilliches/Mansfield approach to economic impact evaluation. See, A.N. Link and J.T. Scott, Evaluating Public Research Institutions, (Routledge) 2005, pp. 103-105.

[3] Gregory Tassey, *The Technology Imperative*, Edward Elgar 2007; *The Roles and Economic Impacts of Technology Infrastructure* (version 3), 2008; and "The disaggregated technology production function: A new model of university and corporate research," *Research Policy*, 34 (2005) 287–303.

[4] See, for example, Trade and the impact of innovations and standards: the case of Germany and the UK, Knut Blind and Andre Jungmittag, *Applied Economics*, 2005, vol. 37, issue 12, pages 1385-1398; Knut Blind, The Economics of Standards: Theory, Evidence, Policy, (publisher)

[5] The ISO is undertaking a study to develop a general methodology for assessing the impact of documentary standards.

[6] David Leech is a Senior Analyst with the Industry & Technology Evaluation Intelligence Group (TASC) of Northrop Grumman Corporation

[7] Joanne Henson was a Guest Researcher at NIST during 2008.

[8] Erik Puskar, *Selected Impacts of Documentary Standards Supported by NIST*, NISTIR 7398, March 2007.

[9] Our approach is adaptation of an approach to strategic assessment developed Clayton M. Christensen, Paul Carlile, and David Sundahl, *The Process of Theory-Building*, (Harvard Business School Working Paper 02-016), 2002; Clayton M.Christensen and Michael E. Raynor, "Why Hard-Nosed Executives Should Care About Management Theory," *Harvard Business Review*, September 2003, pp. 67- 74; and, Paul R. Carlile and Clayton M. Christensen, *The Cycles of Theory Building in Management Research*, (Harvard Business School Working Paper 05-057), 2005.

[10] For example, see, Tassey, op.cit., 2005; and the "U.S. Measurement System" framework described in, Dennis Swyt, *An Assessment of the United States Measurement System*, NIST Special Publication 1048, February, 2007. The United States Measurement System (USMS) is described as an essential infrastructure *woven into the fabric* of our economy by the organizing activities of private sector standards developing organizations (SDOs), supported by NIST's participation in these SDOs and its measurement science and technology development activities. From an economic perspective, these private and public activities mitigate the measurement risks and costs associated with product development, production, marketing, and use.

[11] In the context of the proposed strategic assessment development process, case studies are understood not simply as stand-alone vignettes but rather as means of building towards the kind of rich analysis capability that allows the case study & lessons learned step to transition the strategic assessment step. See, Robert Yin, *Case Study Research Design*, 4th edition, Sage Publications, 2005 [CHECK CITATION]; and Christenson, et al, op. cit., 2002, 2003, 2005.

[12] See, "Essays in Honor of Edwin Mansfield," *The Journal of Technology Transfer*, Vol. 30, Nos. 1/2, January 2005; Cite a compilation of ATP economic assessments; Tassey, op. cit., 2008.

[13] See, John T. Scott, "Financing and Leveraging Public/Private Partnerships: The Hurdle-Lowering Auction," STI Review, No. 23, 1998, pp.67-84.

[14] See, Ruegg, Rosalie and Irwin Feller, "*A Toolkit for Evaluating Public R&D Investment*", NIST, July 2003, p. 34

[15] Nanotechnology (environment, health and safety measures); Biosciences; Leap-ahead security technologies; Optical communications and computing; Neutron research expansion; Quantum science, Enabling nanotechnology; Climate change science program; Measurement science; Earthquake hazards reduction; Disaster resilient structures; Hydrogen as fuel; Biometrics; Supply chain integration.

[16] The fraction of value added from new products or services depends on the gap in the timing or scope of the standards that can be attributed to NIST's participation.

[17] It is possible that in some instances a narrower scope might actually serve the market better, but only 4 percent of the respondents indicated that NIST's involvement narrowed the scope of the standard.

[18] As with the other intermediate indicators, we are only claiming that evidence of industry group or consortium involvement is suggestive of significant benefits. Significant economic impact is a much stronger claim requiring significant net benefits.

[19] Link and Scott distinguish three different approaches to evaluating economic impact: the counterfactual approach, the Grilliches/Mansfield approach, and the spillover approach. The counterfactual approach

Lab	Title	Description	Impact	SDO	Contact	Completed ?
PL/TS	X-Ray Security Screening Systems	NIST is leading a program to develop 4 technical performance standards (ANSI N42.44-47) related to the image quality of x-ray security screening systems for cargo, computerized tomography (for checked baggage), checkpoint and body scan. These standards will include test methods, test artifacts, and minimum performance requirements where this does not compromise security sensitive information.	These standards will be used by DHS and state and local governments to insure that only systems that meet satisfactory levels of performance will be purchased and used in the nation's aviation security venues, public buildings and events, and screening at ports, borders, and prisons.	IEEE /ANSI N42.46 (2008) N42.44 (2008)	Larry Hudson	No, remaining in 2009

ENDNOTES

[1] It is possible that in some instances a narrower scope might actually serve the market better, but only 4 percent of the respondents indicated that NIST's involvement narrowed the scope of the standard.

[2] Link and Scott distinguish three different approaches to evaluating economic impact: the counterfactual approach, the Grilliches/Mansfield approach, and the spillover approach. The counterfactual approach appears more conservative, in the sense that it accounts for first-order net benefits that accrue to NIST's unique contributions. The availability of new products and services suggests second-order benefits and the application of the Grilliches/Mansfield approach to economic impact evaluation. See, A.N. Link and J.T. Scott, Evaluating Public Research Institutions, (Routledge) 2005, pp. 103-105.

[3] Gregory Tassey, *The Technology Imperative*, Edward Elgar 2007; *The Roles and Economic Impacts of Technology Infrastructure* (version 3), 2008; and "The disaggregated technology production function: A new model of university and corporate research," *Research Policy*, 34 (2005) 287–303.

[4] See, for example, Trade and the impact of innovations and standards: the case of Germany and the UK, Knut Blind and Andre Jungmittag, *Applied Economics*, 2005, vol. 37, issue 12, pages 1385-1398; Knut Blind, The Economics of Standards: Theory, Evidence, Policy, (publisher)

[5] The ISO is undertaking a study to develop a general methodology for assessing the impact of documentary standards.

[6] David Leech is a Senior Analyst with the Industry & Technology Evaluation Intelligence Group (TASC) of Northrop Grumman Corporation

[7] Joanne Henson was a Guest Researcher at NIST during 2008.

[8] Erik Puskar, *Selected Impacts of Documentary Standards Supported by NIST*, NISTIR 7398, March 2007.

[9] Our approach is adaptation of an approach to strategic assessment developed Clayton M. Christensen, Paul Carlile, and David Sundahl, *The Process of Theory-Building*, (Harvard Business School Working Paper 02-016), 2002; Clayton M.Christensen and Michael E. Raynor, "Why Hard-Nosed Executives Should Care About Management Theory," *Harvard Business Review,* September 2003, pp. 67- 74; and, Paul R. Carlile and Clayton M. Christensen, *The Cycles of Theory Building in Management Research*, (Harvard Business School Working Paper 05-057), 2005.

[10] For example, see, Tassey, op.cit., 2005; and the "U.S. Measurement System" framework described in, Dennis Swyt, *An Assessment of the United States Measurement System,* NIST Special Publication 1048, February, 2007. The United States Measurement System (USMS) is described as an essential infrastructure *woven into the fabric* of our economy by the organizing activities of private sector standards developing organizations (SDOs), supported by NIST's participation in these SDOs and its measurement science and technology development activities. From an economic perspective, these private and public activities mitigate the measurement risks and costs associated with product development, production, marketing, and use.

[11] In the context of the proposed strategic assessment development process, case studies are understood not simply as stand-alone vignettes but rather as means of building towards the kind of rich analysis capability that allows the case study & lessons learned step to transition the strategic assessment step. See, Robert Yin, *Case Study Research Design*, 4th edition, Sage Publications, 2005 [CHECK CITATION]; and Christenson, et al, op. cit., 2002, 2003, 2005.

[12] See, "Essays in Honor of Edwin Mansfield," *The Journal of Technology Transfer*, Vol. 30, Nos. 1/2, January 2005; Cite a compilation of ATP economic assessments; Tassey, op. cit., 2008.

[13] See, John T. Scott, "Financing and Leveraging Public/Private Partnerships: The Hurdle-Lowering Auction," STI Review, No. 23, 1998, pp.67-84.

[14] See, Ruegg, Rosalie and Irwin Feller, "*A Toolkit for Evaluating Public R&D Investment*", NIST, July 2003, p. 34

[15] Nanotechnology (environment, health and safety measures); Biosciences; Leap-ahead security technologies; Optical communications and computing; Neutron research expansion; Quantum science, Enabling nanotechnology; Climate change science program; Measurement science; Earthquake hazards reduction; Disaster resilient structures; Hydrogen as fuel; Biometrics; Supply chain integration.

[16] The fraction of value added from new products or services depends on the gap in the timing or scope of the standards that can be attributed to NIST's participation.

[17] It is possible that in some instances a narrower scope might actually serve the market better, but only 4 percent of the respondents indicated that NIST's involvement narrowed the scope of the standard.

[18] As with the other intermediate indicators, we are only claiming that evidence of industry group or consortium involvement is suggestive of significant benefits. Significant economic impact is a much stronger claim requiring significant net benefits.

[19] Link and Scott distinguish three different approaches to evaluating economic impact: the counterfactual approach, the Grilliches/Mansfield approach, and the spillover approach. The counterfactual approach

appears more conservative, in the sense that it accounts for first-order net benefits that accrue to NIST's unique contributions. The availability of new products and services suggests second-order benefits and the application of the Grilliches/Mansfield approach to economic impact evaluation. See, A.N. Link and J.T. Scott, Evaluating Public Research Institutions, (Routledge) 2005, pp. 103-105.

[20] Methods for Assessing the Economic Impacts of Government R&D (Planning Report 03-1), NIST, September 2003